Good Housekeeping

D0610212

101
DIY
FIXES

YOUR GUIDE TO QUICK JOBS, REPAIRS & RENOVATIONS

COLLINS & BROWN

First published in the United Kingdom in 2010 by
Collins & Brown
10 Southcombe Street
London
W14 0RA

An imprint of Anova Books Company Ltd

The Good Housekeeping website is
www.allboutyou.com/goodhousekeeping

10 9 8 7 6 5 4 3 2 1

ISBN 978-1-84340-567-2

A catalogue record for this book is available from the British Library.

Illustrations by Beci Orpin
Reproduction by Mission Hong Kong
Printed and bound by Times Offset, Malaysia

This book can be ordered direct from the publisher at www.anovabooks.com

Contents

Painting and Decorating

Home Maintenance

Household Fittings

Outside the Home

Plumbing and Heating

Electrics

Miscellaneous

Introduction

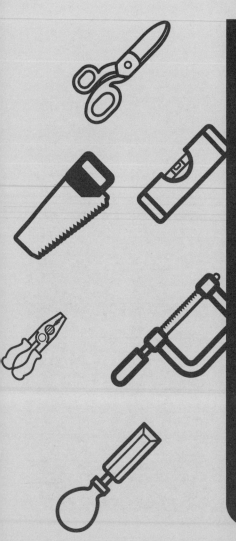

In years past many householders relied on a local tradesman to fix problems in their home. If you needed a new sink, you called the plumber. If you had problems with your guttering, you employed the services of a general building contractor. And if you needed a new plug socket fitted, an electrician would be booked.

However, times have changed. The growth of the DIY superstore has granted the general public access to a whole manner of tools and supplies (often at heavily discounted prices) aimed specifically at the amateur, which were previously only available at trade stores. Of course, equipment and supplies are of little use without know-how. Which is why a succession of television makeover shows have been broadcast to guide the homeowner through the often murky world of home improvement.

Of course, there have also been numerous books published on do-it-yourself work. But unlike many other publications, *101 DIY Fixes* cuts through the often unnecessary details to impart the core knowledge you need to get to the heart of the problem. Whether it's a troublesome leaking tap, loose slates on your roof, blocked pipes, warped floorboards, or poor insulation, this book provides an efficient step-by-step means of resolving it.

But the book is not just a means of fixing problems. *101 DIY Fixes* also offers advice on building or installing elements in your home from scratch. If you wish to fit a new radiator or relocate an existing one, you will learn how to do so in these pages. Similarly, you will discover helpful advice on installing a plug socket, laying wooden decking to enjoy those summer evenings in the garden, fitting skirting boards, and removing an unwanted fireplace.

All novice DIYers have to start somewhere. At first you may feel nervous about fitting a curtain pole (page 103), but as your confidence grows, even seemingly daunting tasks such as building a partition wall (page 48) or laying a solid floor (page 80) will seem like a breeze in due course.

This book is not limited to DIY solutions, either. For even the simplest of DIY tasks, a basic toolkit is a must. So you will find a basic list of tools on pages 10–11. This is not comprehensive, you can add to your kit as you become more proficient and tackle more complex jobs. However, a hammer, screwdrivers, tape measure, spirit level, adjustable spanner and electric drill are a good starting point. At the back of the book you will also discover some much needed advice on safety while you work, and a condensed version of the 2010 Building Regulations so that you know what changes you are (and are not) permitted to make in your home and the approvals required.

So, if you're ready to embrace this new world of DIY, let *101 DIY Fixes* guide you every step of the way. Not only will you find completing these household tasks hugely rewarding, but you will also save a good deal of money.

DIY v BUILDER

DIY is a great way to refurbish your house for a fraction of the cost of a professional tradesman. But despite all the greats tips contained within this book, DIY isn't always the best solution. Learn when to do the job yourself and when to call in a builder.

Assuming that your house is more or less suitable for your needs but you feel its layout or facilities could be improved – and it is in need of a good overhaul in certain departments – what are you going to do?

Basic jobs

In general terms, there are some basic jobs that can be done immediately with few skills and a simple toolkit. Take the doors in a room, for example. Are there too many? Would it be more convenient if one opened outwards into a hallway rather than into a room? Could a sliding or folding door instead of a hinged one save valuable floor space?

Such jobs, involving some ability in the use of bricks or plasterboard needed to block off a doorway or basic screwdriver and chisel work to alter the type or operation of doors, cost very little to do. Even blocking off a window to create a complete run of wall for extra storage requirements is not going to over-tax your purse or your do-it-yourself skills.

Big jobs

The problem you will face in altering walls will depend on whether they are simply of a partitioning or load-bearing nature. The former, especially in a modern house, where many interior walls are of plasterboard construction, is simple to remove. On the other hand, a brick wall serving as a partition can be a daunting task for anyone not used to heavy work.

If the brick wall is load-bearing – that is, supporting part of the house structure above – then it requires expert building knowledge to decide on the correct replacement support to insert before it is demolished. With any work of this sort you must get professional, on-the-spot advice before you do anything.

Conversely, if you need an extra room, it could well be possible to partition off a large room to create two smaller ones. In this case, building a plasterboard wall is essentially a 'hammer and nails' carpentry job that most capable people should well be equal to.

The problem with planning alterations on this scale is being able to take a detached, clinical view of a house you have grown used to. It is sometimes impossible, for example, to imagine that cupboards or a large piece of furniture could be moved to an alternative location in a rearranged layout. We tend to become comfortable with familiar surroundings.

Getting organised

Before resorting to paying for the advice of an architect or surveyor, you need to get all your ideas down on paper. In other words, make a scale drawing of the complete floor area you want to alter. This does not have to be elaborate, but it should be accurate – so use graph paper and work to a convenient scale.

On the plan, mark the outside walls of the house and the position of all doors, windows, drains and other service pipes and cable runs. The interior plan should show whether walls are load-bearing or not. In addition, you must indicate precisely the position of doors and windows, pipes and cable runs inside – in fact, put down as much information as you think will be relevant.

It is only when you have the facts spread out in front of you that you can really begin to understand the existing layout of your house – and, most important, the possible opportunities available for change.

The relevance of marking on the plan doors, windows, services and so on is to let you see at a glance where potential problems may lie and how difficult it is going to be to make particular alterations you may want. For example, a bathroom can pose problems since it has to function entirely around the supply and disposal of water. You cannot simply move it to the other side of the house as you might, say, with a dining room.

Even at the end of this exercise, you may still be baffled as to what can be done. If so, a professional should be able to come up with a series of possible options. Architects and surveyors usually work within a similar scale of fees and at least you should be able to get an idea of what the cost is likely to be simply by making a telephone call either to individual practices or to the head office of the relevant association or society.

You are unlikely to be charged an enormous amount for an initial visit, consultation and outline suggestions. Should you decide to take the matter a stage further and have proper plans drawn up for yourself or a builder, then you must ask what the fee for this will be.

Buying a property

You can run through the same process if you are thinking of buying a property and there is no pressure on you to make a quick purchase. However, you may not have sufficient appreciation or knowledge of building work to make a swift, accurate assessment on a particular property when there is a queue of interested parties also considering buying. In this situation, you can take your professional adviser with you to get an immediate expert opinion on the property.

Your initial response may be that this is a waste of money. But imagine what it could be like to buy a house believing it to be possible to make certain alterations or improvements, only to find out a few months later that you cannot do what you want – or that the cost of what you plan is prohibitively expensive.

TOOLS AND MATERIALS

When you move into your own home for the first time you will need certain basic tools just to keep things running and avoid being dependent on other people. The following is a list of tools that should be acquired as soon as is practical. You can find more detailed information throughout the book.

Adjustable spanner

Get one with a jaw opening of 35mm (1⅓ in). You will find it invaluable.

Drills

Mixed set of HSS twist and masonry drills. A handy set would range from 1.5mm to 6mm (1/20 to ¼ in) and cover most wall plug sizes.

Electric drill

The only expensive item on this list. Buy one with a hammer action. This is a necessity even if you only want to hang a picture or put up shelves. You will, at some time or other, need to drill into masonry and an electric hammer drill is the only practical way to do this.

Electrician's pliers

These are useful for all sorts of jobs as well as any wiring work.

Expanding rule

One marked in both metric and imperial sizes and about 3.5m (12ft) long is useful about the house.

Extension lead

One of about 6m (20ft) with two outlets and a built-in overload device is ideal for your electric drill and other household appliances.

Hammer

Cross-pein or claw. A claw hammer is useful for pulling nails out but a cross-pein makes a better general-purpose tool. The pein is used for starting nails.

Masking tape

A roll of 25mm (1in) wide masking tape has a variety of uses, including tidying coiled cables, marking delicate surfaces on which you don't want to write, wrapping around twist drills to indicate depths and masking paintwork.

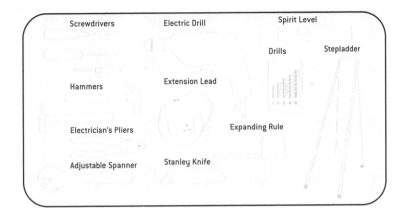

Screwdrivers · Electric Drill · Spirit Level · Drills · Stepladder · Hammers · Extension Lead · Electrician's Pliers · Expanding Rule · Adjustable Spanner · Stanley Knife

Screwdrivers

Buy several. A small slim-bladed one is essential for electric plugs and terminals. A medium slot and medium cross-head should cover immediate needs.

Spirit level

A small handy level will ensure that your shelves are perfectly horizontal.

Stanley knife

With easily replaceable blades, this is useful for cutting vinyl, cork, card and paper.

Stepladders

Indispensable for general household cleaning and maintenance as well as any decorating work.

TOO MANY TOOLS?

Throughout this book you will find constant reference to tools that are required to do this or that job. To kit yourself out with all these tools you would need a second mortgage. These are there mainly to show how a tool designed for a specific purpose and often evolved over many decades can make that particular job easier and more satisfying. Most tools are acquired over a lifetime of tackling different jobs, but also remember to study the list of local tool-hire shops to see what you can hire for short periods.

Painting and Decorating

It's never been easier or more fun to do your own decorating. All you need is a little imagination and some basic know-how to transform your home, help protect it — and save money too. This chapter will tell you everything you need to know, including: the correct way to use a paint brush, how to wallpaper around corners, how to strip wood and how to use special paint effects for that extra-special touch. Your gateway to a new world of DIY starts here.

WHICH PAINT FOR WHICH JOB?

Every year sees the introduction of new, sophisticated paint finishes, such as solid emulsion, one-step gloss, environmentally friendly 'green' paints, and tough sheens for kitchens and bathrooms. But which one is right for the job?

With all these different and confusing products on the market, it may be a relief to know that there are only two main types of house paint: water-based, and solvent-based, which is traditionally, if not always accurately, called oil-based paint.

Water-based paints include emulsion, quick-drying eggshell and water-based gloss, while solvent-based paints range from traditional eggshell and gloss to durable sheen finishes and specialist lacquers or paints for metal. Some paints may have added ingredients such as vinyl, acrylic or polyurethane – to make them more durable or to increase coverage – but that doesn't alter their basic composition.

Water-based paints are ideal for walls and water-based eggshell or gloss can be used for most interior woodwork, while solvent-based paints are perfect for areas of hard wear: exterior as well as interior wood, and metal.

! WATER- OR SOLVENT-BASED?

Find out if a paint is water-based or solvent-based by reading the instructions given for thinning. If water is recommended, the paint will be water-based; if white spirit is advised, it's solvent-based.

Paint disposal

Oil-based paint and solvents are considered hazardous waste materials. They should never be disposed of in the regular rubbish or poured down the sink. Consult your local waste collection department for advice.

Primer

Primer seals absorbent surfaces and provides a key for the subsequent coats. Use it before painting bare timber, and when using gloss on bare metal.

Undercoat

Undercoat provides a smooth, solid-coloured base for liquid gloss. It's a solvent-based paint that looks attractive in its own right, though the range of colours is limited. It tends to chip, so if using it without the top coat of gloss protect it with clear varnish.

Emulsion

Emulsion is the first choice for walls. It's a water-based paint, and normally contains vinyl, which makes it durable and easy to clean. It can be used on most sound, already painted surfaces.

Gloss

Gloss paint is the traditional choice for wood and metalwork. All solvent-based gloss has a high shine but for a truly mirror-like finish, it's best to opt for the liquid paint used over undercoat, a system favoured by professional decorators, especially for outside use.

Eggshell paints

Eggshell is a versatile sheen finish usually sold for indoor woodwork, though it can also be used on walls for a uniform look.

Wood stain

Wood stains designed for use indoors are more decorative than protective, so cover them with two or more coats of clear varnish.

Varnish

Varnish provides a clear, protective coating for paints and stains. It's available in matt, satin (mid-sheen) or high gloss finishes and in liquid or non-drip consistency.

Why not use eco-paints?

They are produced from natural plant oils, resins and minerals so they are non-toxic, healthier to use and better for the environment. They are easy to apply, allow surfaces to breathe and are odour-free.

PAINT SAFETY

Solvent-based paint is flammable, so store it outside the house, but protected from frost and damp.

Fumes from solvent-based gloss and eggshell are unpleasant so make sure the room is cool and well ventilated before you start painting.

PREPARATION FOR PAINTING

Preparation is essential, because paint and paper won't adhere to flaking surfaces and can magnify, rather than disguise, any flaws beneath. As a rule of thumb, allow two-thirds of your time for preparation and one-third for decoration. Clear the room as much as possible, removing light fittings and carpets if you can, and cover what's left with dust-sheets.

Walls

If the walls are in good condition, simply wash them with a detergent solution, rinse and allow to dry.

If the walls are damp, you'll need to find the cause and tackle it before you decorate. Then wash any mould away with a solution of one part bleach to four parts water, leave for two days, and rinse.

Wash walls from the bottom up, to prevent dirty streaks running down and making the task more difficult.

Lift off any patches of flaking plaster, fill dents and cracks, and sand until the repairs are level with the rest of the wall. Don't forget to sand any runs in old paintwork and lightly sand all over walls covered with eggshell or solvent-based paint to provide a key for the next coat. Apply a stabilising solution to thicken powdery plaster, plaster primer to new plaster if necessary, and allow to dry.

Keep it tidy

Keep a pair of old shoes for the job, and leave them by the door of the room being painted when you finish. This will help prevent treading paint and dust through the house when you leave the room.

! PAINT COVERAGE AND DRYING TIMES

TYPE OF PAINT	AREA COVERED PER LITRE	TOUCH DRY	RE-COATABLE
Matt vinyl emulsion	12–14sq m	2 hours	4 hours
Silk vinyl emulsion	12–14sq m	2 hours	4 hours
One-coat emulsion	10sq m	2 hours	4 hours
Liquid gloss	16–17sq m	12 hours	16 hours
Undercoat	15–17sq m	8 hours	12 hours
Masonry paint	6–10sq m	1 hour	4 hours

Woodwork

Before you start, remove all the door furniture (handles, finger plates and so on) and scrape old putty back from the window frames .

If the paintwork is sound, simply sand the surface slightly to provide a key for the new coat, then clean with white spirit. Any blistered or flaking paint should be scraped back and sanded level with the surround.

New wood and bare patches must be primed before painting to seal the surface. This includes the bottom edge of new doors and any deep cracks.

Cracks should be stopped with flexible filler, but if you intend to varnish natural wood, choose a wood filler and stain it to the shade you require.

Treat knots with knotting solution, to prevent resin seeping through and spoiling the new paint. If a knot does bleed through later, sand down to the bare wood, treat with the solution, and then prime before repainting.

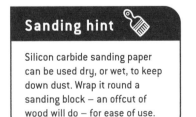

Sanding hint

Silicon carbide sanding paper can be used dry, or wet, to keep down dust. Wrap it round a sanding block – an offcut of wood will do – for ease of use.

How to strip wood

The techniques for preparing wood to give a firm surface for the new coats of paint are the same when working on both the inside and outside of the house.

To strip paint from a windowsill with a hot-air gun, direct it ahead of a shave hook and scrape the paint as soon as it blisters.

Stripping interior woodwork

The areas that will need attention are: doors, windows, skirting boards, stairs and banisters and decorative features such as architraves, picture rails, built-in cupboards, dado rails and wainscotting. There are two ways to strip paint or varnish from wood at home: dry scraping and heat stripping.

DRY SCRAPING

Suitable for small areas only. Scrape the flaking paint off with a hook scraper or a shave hook (the combination shave hook, having a straight and a curved edge, is particularly good on mouldings). Sand the small bare patches level with medium- then fine-grade glasspaper.

HEAT STRIPPING

There are two ways to apply heat to paint: with a blowtorch or an electric hot-air gun.

The second is a fairly recent innovation and although not quite as quick as a torch, is preferable for several reasons: some people are nervous of the flame of a blowtorch, but with a hot-air gun there's no flame, and there's far less likelihood of scorching the wood, which is important if you want to leave the surface bare. When used outdoors, there is no danger of it being extinguished by a sudden gust of wind (although the flex does limit where you can use it; a blowtorch is still hard to beat when working aloft on soffits and fascia boards).

How to use brushes

Brushes should have natural hog's-hair bristles, which pick up more paint than cheaper materials. Look for bristles that don't moult (run them through your hands a few times) and are tapered at the ends for a smooth finish – especially important when painting with eggshell and gloss.

Buy a range of widths (25, 50 and 75mm/ 1, 2 and 3in) for wood and metalwork, plus a 19mm (¾ in) angled cutting-in brush for painting the edge of the wall and a 12mm (½ in) brush for the glazing bars on windows. If you want to paint the walls with a brush, choose a 100mm (4in) wall brush, but make sure it's not too tiring to use.

Clean brushes in detergent for water-based paints, or white spirit for solvent-based.

Ways with brushes

→ Hold a wide brush by the stock – the part that joins the bristles to the handle; hold a narrow one like a pencil.

→ When dipping the brush into the paint, only cover half of the bristle area with emulsion, one-third with gloss. Remove the surplus by pressing the bristles against the side of the tin, not the rim, where paint may dry and lumps may fall into the tin.

→ Tie a length of string tautly across the opening of a paint kettle or paint tin, so you can wipe excess paint off the brush as you lift it out of the paint.

→ For easy cleaning of a brush used with solvent-based paints, drill a hole through the handle of the brush and push a long nail through. Suspend it in a jar of white spirit.

→ When you take a break from painting, wrap brushes in clingfilm so they don't dry out.

→ As soon as you stop for the day, clean brushes in detergent for water-based paints, or white spirit for solvent-based.

How to paint a room

The painting of a room should be approached in a methodical manner, not haphazardly. In order to achieve the best results, follow this advice .

The following steps are the most orderly way to paint a room, and will avoid any drips or spills of one colour or type of paint on another.

1

Paint the ceiling. If there is a ceiling rose or other mouldings, give them an initial coat of paint and complete after finishing the ceiling.

2

Paint the walls, working away from the light source.

3

Paint window frames, picture rail (if any), radiators and doors.

4

Paint the skirting.

Painting a ceiling

Working with your arms above your head can be tiring, so choose a roller or paint pad for fast coverage and, if you can find the colour you want, use solid emulsion (roller paint), which makes less mess. Using extension handles makes access easier but can also affect the way you control the roller. It may be better to work from a plank between two sets of step ladders, but make sure they are stable.

Light work

It's important to work in good light, preferably natural, to ensure even coverage of the paint. If you have to work in artificial light, remove the shade and use a high-wattage bulb.

1

Paint a narrow strip around the perimeter of the ceiling where the roller won't reach, using a narrow 'cutting in' brush.

2

Paint a wider strip parallel to one edge with a wide brush, paint pad or roller, leaving a small gap (see right).

3

When you come to the end of the run, reverse the direction and use the brush, pad or roller to fill in the gap. If necessary, go over it again lightly to blend in the paint .

4

Recharge with paint and start a new line, again leaving a small gap, and continue until the ceiling is complete.

How to paint doors and windows

Doors and windows are the trickiest areas of any room to paint well. This tip instructs you how to avoid any unsightly errors.

Painting windows

When protecting the glass with masking tape, let the paint overlap on to the glass by a millimetre to form a protective seal.

CASEMENT (SIDE OPENING) WINDOWS

1

Paint any glazing bars on the fixed window.

2

Paint the opening window, except for the outside edge, which should match the exterior.

3

Paint the window frame and sill.

Best match

For the best effect, the outside edge of the door should match the paintwork of the room it opens into.

SASH WINDOWS

1

Open the window until the bottom sash and top sash overlap by about 200mm (8in).

2

Paint the bottom of the top sash.

3

Close the bottom sash and pull up the top sash so it's almost closed.

4

Paint the rest of the top sash.

5

Paint the bottom sash.

6

Paint the frame, avoiding the sash cords.

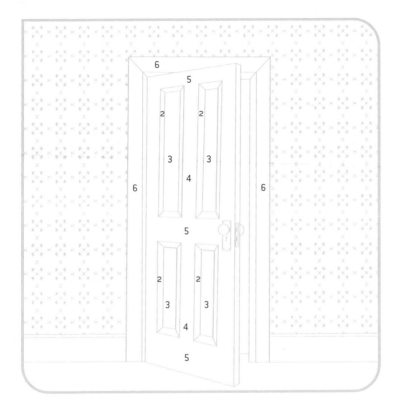

Painting panelled doors

There are six key steps to successful door painting.

1

Remove door 'furniture' (eg, handles, knobs and key plates, etc).

2

Paint the mouldings, if any.

3

Paint the panels.

4

Paint the vertical strips in the centre.

5

Paint the horizontals.

6

Paint the sides, edges and frame.

How to apply paint

Applying paint to a room might at first seem a simple task but if certain rules are not adhered to problems can arise. Paint can be applied either with a brush, roller or, sometimes, a sprayer.

Using a brush

Apply the paint with a wide 100 to 150mm (4 to 6in) brush: dip no more than half of the bristles into the paint and wipe off excess on the edge of the tin. Work across the ceiling, back from the window, in strips 600mm (24in) wide. Turn the brush on its edge to paint a band round the edge of the ceiling, working right into the wall. The overlap will either be covered by paint on the wall or by wallpaper. Then turn the brush full face and proceed to paint in strips. When you're applying emulsion, you're not governed by a strict painting pattern, as it does not readily form solid lines.

Using a roller

A paint roller will speed the operation considerably, which is always welcome, as painting a ceiling is tiring.

Paint a band around the room using a brush: the roller cannot reach into the ceiling/wall angle. To avoid spatters, load the roller with paint and remove the excess by rolling it on the ribbed end of the tray, out of the paint. Keep the roller close to the surface all the time and apply the paint in criss-cross strokes, picking up the wet edges of adjoining star shapes formed to coat the whole area. 'Lay off' by rolling in one direction, parallel to one wall, in very light strokes.

Use a brush on any mouldings and use a brush to apply paint around them.

Spray painting

For exceptional swiftness when painting walls, you'll find a spray gun supreme. Guns can be bought or hired, are either electrically powered or work by pump action and can be used with emulsion or gloss paints.

You'll have to mask off the skirting boards and floor, taping the sheets down with masking tape. The same must be done with switches, sockets and light fittings. Newspaper around the floor close to the walls (over the polythene) will soak up any flying spray.

Apply the paint in horizontal bands but spray the two sides of an interior corner separately. For an even coverage, keep the nozzle at right angles to the wall, 150mm to 200mm (6 to 8in) away, and don't swing it from side to side.

How to paint and varnish woodwork

Applying paint or varnish to woodwork requires a different approach to covering walls and ceiling. This is how to do it.

Painting

When painting wood, brush along the grain. On a narrow area, a single movement will be enough to cover it, but with wide areas, apply paint in parallel bands, reloading the brush before painting each strip. Aim for a smooth flowing movement for even coverage. After painting the second band, paint across the grain to join the two strips. 'Lay off' with light strokes along the grain for a smooth finish. Use two coats of undercoat when covering a dark base – cheaper than an extra coat of gloss.

Hide your mistakes

Make a 'tack rag' – a lint-free cloth moistened with a small amount of white spirit – to erase any mistakes.

Varnishing

If covering a previously varnished or stained surface, sand and clean it. If varnishing bare wood or bare cork, apply a base coat thinned with 10 per cent white spirit.

Dip the brush into the tin of varnish so that half the bristle area is covered, and apply it along the grain, brushing out across the grain from the wet edge for even coverage. There's no pigment in varnish to disguise mistakes, so take care to brush out overlaps and brush marks. Finish by brushing along the grain again with a single smooth stroke.

If more than one coat is needed, lightly sand with very fine abrasive paper when dry and clean with white spirit between each coat.

SPECIAL PAINT EFFECTS

Fashions in decorating are always changing. Plain walls will be popular one year, patterns the next. Decorative paint finishes have the advantage of camouflaging defects and adding interest without defined pattern. You can buy special textured rollers that add a design for you, but it's often just as easy to use traditional materials. Here's what to do.

Walls

COLOUR WASHING

This treatment gives a translucent finish. Paint the wall with solvent-based eggshell (white will give a delicate effect) and leave to dry. For the top coat, mix 30 per cent transparent oil glaze with 50 per cent solvent-based eggshell and 20 per cent white spirit. If you want solid cover and a formal effect, use it straight; for a more casual, random effect, apply with a wall brush, moving it in all directions and leaving some areas uncovered to vary the depth of colour. Repeat when dry, covering the entire wall, still using criss-cross brush strokes.

You can protect the finish with a coat of polyurethane varnish in areas of hard wear but this will need to be removed when repainting.

BEST FOR cottagey living rooms, dining rooms and bedrooms.

Top Tip

A similar effect can be achieved with emulsion paint. Paint the wall and leave to dry, then apply two coats of emulsion thinned with water, following the instructions on the tin. Use a wall brush, not a roller, and apply the paint with a random movement.

SPONGING

An easy technique with emulsion paint, although solvent-based eggshell, which takes longer to dry, gives more time to create an effect. For the best results, use related colours, sponging the deeper colour over the paler one or vice versa. (Use three colours if you want a more elaborate effect.)

Pour a little paint into a saucer and apply with a natural sea sponge in a random direction, turning the sponge from time to time, until the wall is covered. You can use rags instead of a sponge if you prefer, choosing a textured cloth such as stockinette or cheesecloth for greater definition.

BEST FOR bedrooms and bathrooms.

RAG ROLLING

This needs a base coat of solvent-based eggshell and a top coat made from 70 per cent transparent oil glaze, 20 per cent eggshell and 10 per cent white spirit. Working from the top of the wall down, this is brushed on in vertical bands and rolled off with rags twisted into a sausage-shape.

BEST FOR dining rooms and bedrooms.

STIPPLING

The subtlest way of producing broken colour. Paint the wall with solvent-based eggshell and, when dry, apply with a special stippling brush a top coat made from 70 per cent transparent oil glaze, 20 per cent eggshell and 10 per cent white spirit. Keep the bristles at right angles to the wall, and wipe them from time to time so they don't become clogged.

You can also stipple walls by painting narrow (50cm/20in) strips of the top coat from top to bottom and then removing colour by using a clean, dry stippling brush.

For speed, pour the top coat into a roller tray and apply with a stiff brush.

BEST FOR all around the house.

STENCILLING

Stencilling can create attractive borders and decorative motifs. Cutting your own stencils takes practice, so it's easiest to use ready-made stencils, available from most DIY superstores and decorating shops (such as Laura Ashley) as well as specialist suppliers such as The Stencil Store. Whatever you choose, start with relatively simple designs, especially if you're stencilling a border, which can be time-consuming. Add variety by reversing the stencil from time to time, but to avoid smudges, remember to wipe it clean before you turn it over.

Use a stubby stencil brush and dab colour into the stencil until the design is filled in. You can use a variety of paints, from standard emulsion or eggshell (use solvent-based on woodwork) to acrylic or spray paint; special crayons are also available.

BEST FOR borders, ceiling decorations, and motifs on furniture.

Top Tip

Fix the stencil in place with masking tape or spray photo-mount, not Blu-Tack, which leaves a gap between the stencil and the wall and may lead to runs.

MURALS

Murals can be painted in sections using simple picture-book designs.

Draw a grid over the original picture and number the squares, then draw a similar grid, the size of the finished mural, on the wall. Copy the outline of the design into each square, using chalk or soft pencil, then fill in, using one colour at a time and working from the top down. Rub off the grid marks when the mural is dry.

BEST FOR passages and children's bedrooms.

Woodwork

COLOUR RUBBING

This gives a faded, weathered look. It involves brushing a milky glaze or a thin wash of water-based paint over the surface and then removing the excess before it dries, to highlight mouldings or emphasise the grain.

Alternatively, apply a base coat of solvent-based eggshell or wipe the bare wood with white spirit, and make a glaze from 75 per cent transparent oil glaze, 20 per cent solvent-based eggshell and 5 per cent white spirit. Brush this into the surface so that all the crevices are filled, and when it becomes tacky, rub along the grain with a soft cloth.

BEST FOR doors, decorative fireplaces and floors (but not floors subject to hard wear).

MARBLING

Paint with off-white solvent-based eggshell and, when dry, add a top coat made from 30 per cent transparent oil glaze, 50 per cent bone colour eggshell and 20 per cent white spirit. Dab with a rag to soften the effect and, while still wet, trace in the marble 'veins' in dark grey, using an artist's paint brush. For a natural effect, blur the lines with a special softening brush (or improvise with a rag) .

BEST FOR table tops and floors.

WOODGRAINING

A way to make chipboard and pine look like oak or mahogany.

Give softwood and fibreboard a coat of woodfiller thinned to the consistency of single cream, and sand when dry. Repeat this step, then paint with primer, undercoat and red-brown eggshell. (Make sure it's solvent-based.)

Mix several small batches of 60 per cent transparent oil glaze, 20 per cent eggshell and 20 per cent white spirit in progressively deeper shades of brown. Apply along the grain, starting with the lightest colour, using a comb or a special graining brush, and blur for a natural effect with a cloth or softening brush. Finish with button polish or polyurethane.

BEST FOR small pieces of furniture, hand rails and panelling.

PAINTING TROUBLESHOOTING

If you're a novice painter there are several pitfalls you might encounter. Forewarned is forearmed is ...

Blisters are often caused by painting damp wood. Allow the paint to harden, then prick the blister. If it's wet inside, you'll need to strip back and fill the grain before repainting.

Crazing is caused by applying a second coat before the first coat is dry. Allow to dry, then rub down and repaint.

Cratering comes from too much damp in the atmosphere. Sand and repaint, keeping the room warm and dry.

Flaking paint is caused by powdery or dirty walls underneath the new coat, or gloss paint that hasn't been sanded. Emulsion paint often flakes off woodwork and radiators, so rub it down and repaint with a coat of solvent-based eggshell or gloss.

Runs comes from overloading the brush. If there are only one or two, allow the paint to dry completely and then prick, rub down and touch in with a small paintbrush. Alternatively, sand and start again.

Show through of what was originally underneath needs an additional top coat (emulsion) or an undercoat plus a new top coat (gloss).

Specks and stray bristles can be avoided if both wall and paint are clean and you use quality brushes. Either sand down and start again or, in a small area, sand or pick out the pieces, rub with wet abrasive paper and touch in. This also works for insects that have been trapped in wet paint.

Uneven coverage may occur if you try to spread paint too thinly or fail to prime large patches of filler or bare plaster. These are more absorbent than the rest of the wall and so take in more paint than primed areas.

PREPARATION FOR WALLPAPERING

Any lumps and bumps on the walls are likely to show through wallpaper just as they do through paint, so walls should be filled and sanded smooth. Old wallpaper should be stripped away because it's rarely a satisfactory surface for the new layer. Wrinkles will be repeated, colour may bleed through, and the weight of the new paper may pull it all away from the wall.

Stripping wallpaper

1

Vinyls and paper-backed wallpapers are often designed for dry stripping, which means they can be peeled away from the backing. Try lifting a corner and pulling upwards and outwards (see right). The backing can be used as lining paper if it's in good condition, especially if you intend to paint over the top or want to cover it with heavy wallpaper.

2

To remove standard wallpaper, first turn off the electricity at the mains. Then wet the wallpaper with detergent solution, working from the top of the wall down so the water runs over the wallpaper, giving it a chance to penetrate. (Be careful not to over-wet if you're working on plasterboard.)

3

If the wallpaper is coated or overpainted, you'll probably need to scrape the surface with a wire brush before wetting it to improve absorbency. Leave it to soak before you try to remove the wallpaper.

4

It's often worth hiring or buying a steam wallpaper stripper, which can speed things up if there are several layers of paper to remove (below).

5

Using a scraper with a wide blade, start at the seams and base. With luck, you'll be able to remove a sizeable strip of wallpaper, but try not to damage the wall beneath, as any chips will need to be filled.

When all the paper has been removed, finish by sanding lightly to remove any small pieces of paper still stuck to the walls.

Planning papering

Ideally, you should start in a corner and work away from the light so that the joins between lengths are less noticeable. Before you start, it's worth marking where the joins will fall and adjusting your starting point if lengths meet in a prominent place. As a rule, where there are no special features, and unless you are left-handed, start at the wall to the right of the main window and work around the room.

However, if there is a chimney breast, paste the first length in the middle of it. Treat each half of the room separately, working towards the door and starting at the chimney breast again to paper the other side. This way, awkward joins can be minimised.

Adhesives

Standard wallpaper paste (available as powder or ready-mixed) is suitable for light and medium-weight wallpapers but heavy wallpaper needs a heavy-duty paste.
Vinyls and plastic-coated wallpapers need a fungicidal adhesive to prevent mould.

How to hang wallpaper

Wallpapering is a specialist skill. For the novice DIY enthusiast there are many potential things that can go wrong – from overpasting the paper, to a crinkled finish. Follow these tips to guarantee wallpapering to a professional standard on your very first attempt.

YOU WILL NEED

Copydex or similar adhesive (for repairs)

Paper-hanger's brush

Paper-hanger's shears

Paste brush

Pasting table

Pencil

Plumb bob and line

Ruler or tape measure

Seam roller (to press down wallpaper edges)

Wallpaper paste and bucket

1

Using paper-hanger's shears, cut sufficient drops for about a wall at a time, adding 50–75mm (2–3in) to the length of each drop to allow for trimming at the ceiling and skirting, and matching the pattern as you go. (If there's a substantial pattern repeat, drops will vary in length.)

2

Roll the lengths against the curl to flatten them and then turn them over so that the pasting side is uppermost.

3

Mix the paste as instructed and brush it down the centre of the wallpaper with a pasting brush. (Tie a taut string across the bucket to remove excess paste from the brush.) Brush the paste out from the centre, first away from you and then towards you, so that the edges are covered (see opposite, top).

Ready-pasted wall covering simply needs soaking in water in the trough provided and can be smoothed into place with a sponge. Apply Copydex to seams and edges if they have a tendency to lift.

4

Move the paper up and gently fold the paper over so the pasted surfaces meet. When you have pasted the whole drop, fold the other side so that the top and bottom meet in the centre. (When papering stairways and ceilings, you may have to concertina the paper to paste the longest lengths.)

5

Vinyls can be put up straight away but you should leave standard wallpaper to soak for five minutes and heavier relief designs for ten, so that the paper stretches and bubbles won't occur.

6

To make sure you hang the paper straight, find the vertical, using a plumb bob and line (a small weight on a string) as a guide. Mark a line 25mm (1in) less than the wallpaper's width if you're starting at a corner (because you'll be turning this amount on to the adjacent wall) and hang the first piece of wallpaper, using this line as a guide, allowing about 70mm (2¾in) to overlap on the ceiling and 25mm (1in) to turn round the corner.

7

Manoeuvre the top half into place and smooth down with a paper-hanger's brush, pushing it well into the corner (see right, middle). Release the bottom half, lower gently (it may stretch if dropped) and smooth into place. Mark a fold at skirting and ceiling level with the shears and trim to fit (see right, below).

8

Hang the next length so it butts tightly up to the first, because the paper will shrink as it dries. Leave for five minutes and then press into place with a seam roller.

TRICKY AREAS

Many people find wallpapering hard enough when dealing solely with large flat walls. However, there are also awkward areas such as ceilings, corners and light switches to overcome. But with a little know-how these needn't be a problem for you.

Ceilings

Paste the paper and fold into a concertina, then unfold as you press into place. Smooth down with a broom; this is best done by a partner walking behind you.

Corner

Unless the gap between the previous length of paper and the corner of the room is very narrow, cut the last length on the wall so that it turns the corner by about 25mm (1in). Find the vertical on the new wall and hang the first length on that wall so that it covers the overlaps. External (convex) corners (on alcoves and chimney breasts, for example) may need a larger overlap to make sure seams don't coincide with the exposed corners, where they will almost certainly tear.

Top Tip

'Feather' relief papers to make the edge thinner by tearing the edge and pressing down with a seam roller to minimise bulk when overlapping a corner.

Fixings

Insert matches to mark the site of screws or picture hangers and allow them to pierce through the wallpaper when you smooth it into place.

Light switches

Turn off the electricity and remove the switch cover. Hang the wallpaper over the switch and smooth into place. Cut away a square of wallpaper 6mm (¼ in) less than the size of the switch, then replace the cover, tucking in the edges. If the switch projects, cut an X shape in the paper across it and trim the wallpaper, leaving a small margin to overlap on to the sides of the cover (see right). Always use this technique with foil wall coverings, which conduct electricity and must not be tucked under the switch cover.

Stairways

Start with the longest drop, marking the vertical by fixing a piece of chalked string from top to bottom of the stair well, and snapping it against the wall. Cut each length separately, matching the pattern and making sure that the length is sufficient to take in the angled skirting (see right).

Windowsills

Pull the paper over the corner of the sill and slit it before smoothing the paper into place.

How to hang borders

Borders are available in wallpaper or ready-pasted vinyl, but though pasting techniques may differ, they are cut and fixed in more or less the same way.

YOU WILL NEED

Same equipment as for hanging wallpaper plus a spirit level

How to mitre a border

1 Find the right-hand vertical with a plumb bob and line and mark with a pencil, then paste a strip of border into place, allowing 25mm (1in) more than the finished size.
2 Check the horizontal with a spirit level and smooth the border across the top of the panel into place, allowing another 25mm (1in) overlap on the right-hand side.
3 Mitre the corner by placing a ruler across the diagonal from the outer to the inner edge and cut along this line with a trimming knife. Take off the surplus triangle on top, then peel back the horizontal border and remove the excess from beneath. Smooth the edges into place.

1

Mark the position of the border lightly in pencil, using a spirit level to find the horizontal. Then step back and see how it looks to the eye. It's sometimes better to have a border that follows the walls or ceiling than one that emphasises irregularities.

2

Cut the border, and paste or soak it.

3

Concertina the folds, matching pasted edge to pasted edge, and unwind carefully, smoothing into place as you go.

4

Butt-join ends, making sure the pattern matches, and press the margins down firmly.

WALLPAPERING TROUBLESHOOTING

As with painting, there are several problems that can beset anyone with limited experience of wallpapering. Pay attention to the following five areas and, above all, try to stay focused on the job in hand.

Bubbles form if the wallpaper isn't pasted thoroughly or isn't given time to soak. They can also occur if the length isn't smoothed out properly. It's sometimes possible to slit air bubbles with a razor blade and paste the edges into place.

Dirty marks can usually be removed with a white eraser (use with care) or a piece of stale white bread.

Gaps can appear if lengths are not pushed together or if the paper has been stretched too much when smoothed out and has shrunk back when dry.

Peeling is often caused by damp. If it's not substantial, try lifting and re-pasting the edges with wallpaper paste or Copydex.

Tears may not be noticeable if they're stuck down carefully.

TOP TIP

Use a seam roller with care on relief wallpaper as it may crush the design.

Pattern matching

Straight-match wallpapers line up horizontally. Drop-match wallpapers require adjoining lengths to be moved up or down to match up. Random (free-match) designs don't need to be pattern matched. Pattern repeats can make a difference to the amount of wallpaper you need. Remember to allow extra when estimating quantity.

Home
Maintenance

Armed with a sound knowledge of painting and decorating, you are probably eager to tackle more complex tasks. This chapter provides comprehensive instruction for a range of DIY jobs inside the home, from the relative basics of repairing wall cracks, to blocking in a doorway, fitting coving, laying floor tiles and removing a fireplace. Tackling these jobs yourself, rather than hiring professional help, will save you a considerable amount of money and give you a huge sense of satisfaction.

TIP 16

How to repair wall cracks

Small cracks and holes in the surface of internal walls are the result of such things as natural movement, knocks, drying plaster, passing traffic and slamming doors. If you are planning to paint or wallpaper a wall with such imperfections, it is essential first to fill the crack and smooth it over.

1

Open up small cracks with a putty knife or the end of a screwdriver to make them easier to fill.

2

Dampen with a small paintbrush dipped in water to clean out the crack and remove the dust.

3

Apply filler (available ready-mixed or in powder form) with a narrow-bladed filling knife, pushing it deeply into the crack so it fills it completely and leaving it raised above the level of the wall. (Deep cracks must be filled in layers, leaving each to dry before you add the next.)

4

When dry, sand the area down until it's flush with the wall and wipe clean.

Large cracks

These can be repaired using proprietary fillers, building them up in layers as described above. For particularly large holes, however, these fillers will prove expensive to use.

On solid walls a cheaper option is to use conventional plaster. Chip away all the loose material and brush out the dust. Then, with an old brush or hand-held sprayer, wet the area and apply an undercoat. As soon as this has set, apply a top coat of finishing plaster, which you smooth on using a steel float.

Be flexible

Choose a flexible sealant for cracks between walls and window or door frames, which may expand or contract. If you use ordinary filler, the crack may open again.

How to repair plasterboard

If the hole is in a plasterboard wall the techniques you need are somewhat different. Where the holes in plasterboard walls are small, the use of an ordinary filler should do the job. But larger holes will have to be patched.

Basic repair

Use a trimming knife to cut back the damaged board to leave a clean outline. Then prepare an offcut of plasterboard slightly wider than the hole and use this to fill behind the hole.

To help you position this offcut, make two holes in it and feed some string through them, leaving the two end lengths hanging so you can use them to hold the offcut while you position it.

Apply some fresh plaster or filler around the edges on the face of the offcut. Then, keeping hold of the string, pass the offcut through the hole and pull it up behind. Leave it like this until the plaster has set. Pull out the string or cut it off, then fill the hole in the normal way. When the filler has hardened, skim over the repair with a little more filler for a flush finish.

Large holes

In the case of a large hole, it may be better to fill the majority of it with a scrap of plasterboard over the previously fixed offcut using wet plaster. When dry, you simply have to fill the remaining cracks around the edge of the repair and possibly finish off with a skim coat of plaster over the whole surface.

For very large holes, it will be better to cut out a rectangle of plasterboard to expose the timber studs at each side of the damaged area. Then fix a new section of plasterboard to the studs with galvanised nails. Use joint filler to repair the crack around the patch.

Position the offcut in the hole.

Lath and plaster

If the hole is in a lath and plaster wall, cut the plaster away to expose the laths. If these are broken, fold a piece of expanded metal mesh over the sounds laths at the top and bottom of the hole and then replaster.

Once filled, cut the string.

Smooth over for a professional finish.

TIP 18

How to patch loose plaster

If a plastered wall sounds hollow when you tap — and often there will be a surface bulge as well — the plaster is said to have 'blown', which means that it has come away from the undersurface. This is a common problem in older houses.

If you find blown plaster on a solid wall, again you will have to cut back all the loose material until you reach sound plaster. Extensive replastering could be required. If half the wall or more is affected and you do not feel particularly confident about plastering, a sensible solution would be to hack off all the plaster and 'dry-line' the wall with plasterboard.

1

To replaster a large area, brush down the brick or blockwork to remove any remaining dust or debris, then dampen the wall.

2

Use a lightweight browning plaster as the undercoat and mix this with water to make it smooth and easy to apply.

Starting at the bottom of the wall, load the steel float and apply the plaster firmly to the wall with an upward stroke. Continue in this way, building up the thickness to just below the surface level of the sound surrounding plaster.

3

Use a long length of timber held on edge to pull over the replastered area to check there are no high spots.

4

As soon as the undercoat has hardened you can apply the finishing coat, again using the trowel. Pull a straight-edge over the surface to ensure no high spots. Smooth the surface with a steel float and, as soon as the plaster has hardened, dampen the surface with water. Then polish it smooth and flat with the float.

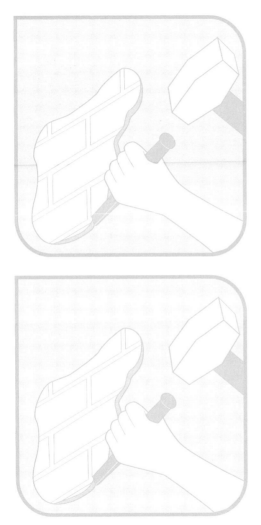

To patch areas of loose plaster, cut back the area until sound plaster is reached. Then apply new plaster with a float, rule it off with a batten flush with the surrounding wall surface, and polish it off with the float.

TIP 19

How to remove a wall

If you want to gain extra space, it may be possible to remove a dividing wall and so knock two rooms into one. Remember that you must obtain local authority approval before doing this. You will have to supply structural calculations to show that the lintel you must install above the opening will support the load.

If the wall is non-loadbearing, a lintel will only have to support the weight of the wall above the opening. If it is loadbearing, a substantial lintel will be required to support the other parts of the building.

Props

Basically, the job involves cutting holes in the wall above the proposed lintel position so that the wall can be temporarily supported on timber beams, known as needles, held up with adjustable steel props, which you can hire. With a loadbearing wall, two sets of props will be needed. One set supports the wall as described above, while the other set is placed under the ceiling to support the upper floor joists, which run at right angles to the wall.

Ceiling height

If the room has a high ceiling, the holes for the needles can be knocked through the wall just under the ceiling above the planned position of the lintel.

If the room has a low ceiling, some floorboards will have to be removed in the room above the opening to allow the props to pass through and support the needles, which are positioned to support the wall upstairs. This allows the lintel to be positioned immediately below the floor joists to give maximum headroom.

Demolition

With the wall and floor well supported, the wall can be demolished and brick piers built up at each side of the room to support the lintel. The blocks on each side that will bear the lintel must be very carefully levelled. When set, the lintel can be lifted into place on them.

Making good

The next stage is to make good the wall above the lintel by bricking up around the needles. When the new brickwork has set, the needles are removed and the holes bricked up. Finally, the whole area is plastered.

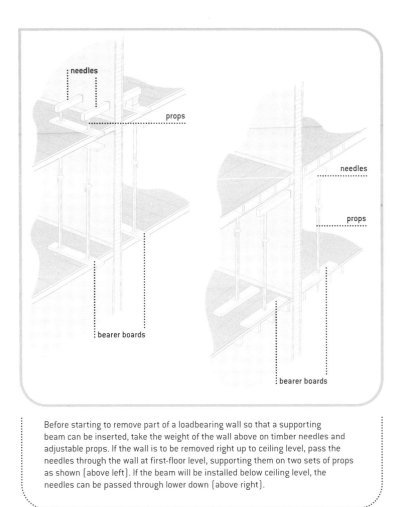

Before starting to remove part of a loadbearing wall so that a supporting
beam can be inserted, take the weight of the wall above on timber needles and
adjustable props. If the wall is to be removed right up to ceiling level, pass the
needles through the wall at first-floor level, supporting them on two sets of props
as shown (above left). If the beam will be installed below ceiling level, the
needles can be passed through lower down (above right).

How to build a partition wall

If you want to divide a large room, the easiest way is to build a stud partition wall. This involves make a framework of 75 x 50mm (3 x 2in) timber studs, clad on both sides with sheets of plasterboard.

1

The first stage is to screw a length of timber (called the sole plate) to the floor at the wall position. Mark plumb lines up the side walls to ascertain the corresponding position on the ceiling and then fix another length of timber (the head plate) to the ceiling. The screws holding the head plate should go into the ceiling joists, which you can find by probing with a thin screwdriver.

2

Next, screw the end studs (vertical timbers) to the side walls between the head and sole plates. Decide on the door position, remove a section of the sole plate and fix studs at each side, using rebated housing joints in the head plate for a secure fixing. Allow for the thickness of the timber lining that will frame the door.

Fix further studs at 400mm (16in) centres by skew-nailing them to the head and sole plates. Three studs should support each 1200mm (4ft) wide plasterboard sheet.

3

Next, nail the noggins (horizontal timbers) between the studs at about 1200mm (4ft) centres. You will need a noggin at the top of the door frame and you can fix additional noggins as required to form windows in the wall. This may be necessary, for example, to allow 'borrowed' light into one room from the adjoining one.

4

At this stage you should run any services, such as plumbing pipes or electrical cables, within the framework of the wall. Then cover the wall with sheets of tapered-edge plasterboard, fixing them with plasterboard nails at 150mm (6in) intervals.

5

Cover up all nail head depressions and joints with filler. While this is still wet, press joint tape into the filler and smooth off. Apply further filler as a wide band over the tape and feather off the edges using a damp sponge.

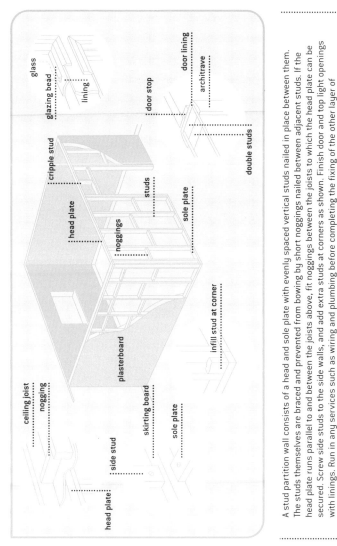

head plate

ceiling joist
nogging
side stud
skirting board
sole plate
plasterboard
infill stud at corner

head plate
cripple stud
glass
glazing bead
lining
noggings
studs
sole plate
door stop
door lining
architrave
double studs

A stud partition wall consists of a head and sole plate with evenly spaced vertical studs nailed in place between them. The studs themselves are braced and prevented from bowing by short noggings nailed between adjacent studs. If the head plate runs parallel to and between the joists above, fit noggings between the joists to which the head plate can be secured. Screw side studs to the side walls, and add extra studs at corners as shown. Finish door and top light openings with linings. Run in any services such as wiring and plumbing before completing the fixing of the other layer of plasterboard cladding.

How to block in a doorway

Blocking up a doorway, like building a partition wall, might sound like a daunting prospect for a DIY job, but it is a relatively simple procedure when you know how.

1

First, remove the door and lining or frame by sawing through and prising off the lengths of timber. With a stud partition wall, the best way to block the opening is to fix an additional timber frame in the gap and clad both sides with plasterboard, fixing the board grey side outwards. You can then skim over the plasterboard with finishing plaster to bring the surface level with the adjacent walls.

2

With a brick or block wall, you can use the same method, but it is better to block the opening with a similar material to that used for the wall construction. In this case there will be less chance of differential movement causing cracking that would later highlight the presence of the infill.

Remove the door frame and chop out half bricks or blocks at approximately 300mm (12in) intervals so that the bricks or blocks being used to fill the opening will key into the walls at either side.

3

When you have bricked up the opening and the mortar has set, apply an undercoat of browning plaster and then skim over with finishing plaster, levelling it off flush with the original walls on either side.

Making a new doorway

Creating a new doorway requires a considerable amount of planning before work begins. You should also seek the approval of your local Building Control Officer (BCO), as the job must comply with the building regulations. A lintel must be chosen to match the type of wall being cut into and you must select a position for the door that won't interfere with existing cable and pipe runs and is at least 450mm (18in) from any corner.

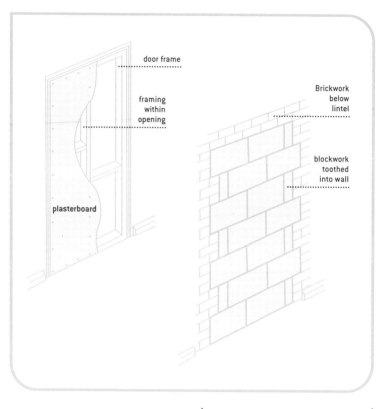

door frame

framing
within
opening

plasterboard

Brickwork
below
lintel

blockwork
toothed
into wall

Block off an unwanted doorway
with a timber framework fixed to
the door frame and covered on both
sides with plasterboard, or remove
the frame and fill the opening with
blockwork.

How to fit a plasterboard ceiling

A new plasterboard ceiling can be fitted directly under the existing one. But you will probably have to screw the new sheets in place. By hammering in nails, you could well shake down the original material. It is much better to pull down the old ceiling and replace it with new sheets of plasterboard nailed directly to the ceiling joists.

Pulling down an old ceiling is messy, but not difficult. Wear old clothes, a hat, dust mask and safety spectacles. Open all the windows in the room and tape round the door to prevent dust from drifting to other parts of the house.

1

Take down the old ceiling using a hammer and cold chisel or a wrecking bar, which is a small crowbar. This usually has a nail-puller at one end and this is ideal for removing nails from the joists. If this proves difficult, drive the nails into the timber instead.

2

If you are replacing the ceiling using plasterboard nailed to the undersides of the joists, use tapered-edge board in the smallest sizes available. Plasterboard is heavy and awkward to lift.

3

Start in one corner and fix the first sheet so that its length is at right angles to the direction of the joists. It will probably be necessary to trim the board so that its end falls midway across a joist. Fix it in place with galvanised large-head plasterboard nails with the cream-coloured face of the board downwards. Insert the nails 150mm (6in) apart and drive them in so that their head just dimples the surface of the board but does not tear it.

4

Cut subsequent sheets so that the joints between the ends of the sheets do not line up. You should butt the long paper-covered edges together, but keep the short cut edges at the ends about 3mm (¹/₁₀in) apart. Fill nail heads and finish the joints with filler and paper joint tape.

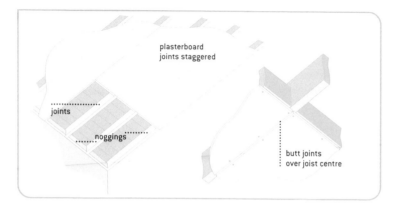

plasterboard
joints staggered

joints

noggings

butt joints
over joint centre

Plasterboard sheets are nailed directly to the undersides of the joists with galvanised nails. Adjacent boards are butt-jointed along the centre line of each joist, and board positions are staggered in adjacent rows. The joints are taped over before the ceiling is given a skim of finishing plaster.

TYPES OF CEILING

There are four basic types of ceiling construction, depending on the style and age of the property. Check which one is used in your house since it can affect the type of problem the ceiling has and therefore the repair work that might be required.

→ Plasterboard – this is nailed directly to the ceiling joists.

→ Lath and plaster – the traditional way of finishing ceilings. Timber laths are nailed to the joists with a narrow gap between them.

→ Timber or boarded – matching tongue and grooved timber boards can look attractive when stained or varnished.

→ Suspended –often formed of a light metal framework forming a grid, which is hung from the original ceiling by wires to lower the height.

How to fit coving

Plaster or rigid plastic coving around the wall and ceiling join provides a neat finish to the room as well as sealing off those awkward and unsightly cracks that always appear. Many homeowners consider fitting coving to be a tricky job that requires a professional tradesman to do well, but by following these instructions you will feel confident enough to tackle it as your next DIY project.

1

First, pencil a guide line, the width of the coving, around the top of the walls and the perimeter of the ceiling.

2

Cut lengths of coving as required to fit, mitring the corners at 45 degrees to ensure a neat, snug fit. Use a mitre box for this or the template that is sometimes supplied. All types of coving can be cut with a fine tooth saw. Remove burrs from rough edges with abrasive paper.

Coving secret

For best results, first fit a length of coving into place at one corner of the room. Then fit a second length at the other end of the same wall. Then fit square-ended lengths in between.

3

Spread coving adhesive on the fixing edges and press the coving in place so that it is aligned with the pencil guide lines. The adhesive should hold the coving. If, however, the wall is uneven, you can temporarily hold it in place with masonry pins until the adhesive has set. These can be pulled out later and the holes filled.

4

Remove excess adhesive with a damp cloth while it is still wet. You can also use the adhesive for making good any gaps between the coving and the walls or ceiling and between adjacent lengths. If using expanded polystyrene coving, you can smooth over the surface using a fine surface filler, which should be rubbed down lightly when dry.

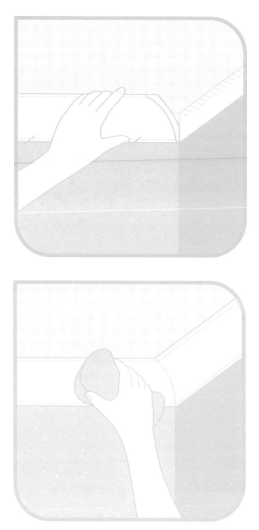

Cut a mitre joint on one end of the first length, butter adhesive on to its rear surfaces and press it into place in one corner of the room.

Wipe off any excess adhesive along the lengths and at joints.

How to restore tiles

After a number of years, the grouting between ceramic tiles in your bathroom and kitchen will become discoloured and spoil the overall effect of what was once a clean, shining surface. By freshening up the tile joints, you can give these areas a real facelift, so that they look like new again.

Replacing grouting

If the grouting is in poor condition, rake it out with a suitably thin sharp tool, such as an old hacksaw blade. This can be a tedious operation. Then replace it with new waterproof grouting. Mix this according to the manufacturer's instructions, which may include a standing period before use.

Apply the new grouting with a plastic spreader, making sure you work it thoroughly into all the gaps. Allow it to dry and then wipe off the surplus with a damp cloth. If you find that you have left too much in some gaps, wait until it is dry and then even it off with a piece of dowelling or similar material.

Painting grouting

If the grouting is in good condition but stained, you can paint it with a special preparation available in a range of colours to match or blend in with your tiles.

Sealant

The gap around the bath and the washbasin should be properly sealed to prevent water getting in behind the fittings. Existing seals will age and break up or become discoloured. The best solution is to remove them and use one of the special silicone rubber sealants now available in a variety of colours to suit your bathroom suite. They are applied straight from the dispenser and full instructions are given as to their application. However, the compound is very sticky and difficult to remove once it has cured and so you must remove any excess immediately.

Because these sealants remain flexible, they are able to accommodate any movement in the fittings without cracking. The problem is that after a time black mould tends to form on them. The easiest way to deal with this is to cut out the old sealant with a sharp cutting knife and reseal the offending section.

How to lay tiles

Tiling can be a complicated job – it is easy to break tiles when cutting them – and is sometimes best left to an expert, especially if a tradesman is already renovating parts of your bathroom. However, follow these instructions to learn to tile yourself and save the cost of employing a contractor.

Types of tile

'Universal' tiles have at least two glazed edges, so you can use them anywhere, turning the glazed edges to the outside when you reach the end of a run. Bevelled-edge universal tiles butt together, leaving a space for the grout and so you won't need to use spacers.

Field tiles have unglazed edges for use in the centre of a panel. They may be self-spacing, with lugs on each side.

Border or edge tiles have one or two rounded edges, to finish the outside of a panel.

Quadrant tiles are narrow rounded strips, used to top standard tiles.

YOU WILL NEED

Grout

Hammer

Metal rule

Nails or tacks

Notched tile-adhesive spreader (often supplied with the tile adhesive)

Pincers for cutting random shapes (if necessary)

Plastic tile spacers or matchsticks (if necessary)

Sand paper (for stripping)

Spirit level

Sponge

Tile adhesive

Tile file

Tungsten carbide tile cutter

Wooden battens

TIP 25

1

Before tiling, wash down emulsion paint and sand solvent-painted surfaces to provide a key. Strip off all wallpaper.

2

Work out where the cut tiles will fall. Have a 'dry run' and readjust if there are any very narrow pieces to cut at the end of a run. It's better to have two symmetrically cut tiles at each end.

3

Measure the distance of one tile up from the skirting or work-top and find the true horizontal with a spirit level. Mark with a pencil and nail or tack a slim wooden batten to the wall along this line.

4

Check the vertical with a spirit level and fix a batten at the end of the last full row of tiles, to keep the tiles in line (below).

Top Tip

You can tile over old tiles if you rub down and seal with plaster primer to provide a key. You'll need a wooden strip or pieces of tile to conceal the double thickness at the top.

5

Starting in the corner where the battens meet, spread tile adhesive on to a square metre of wall, combing it with a notched spreader until it is even.

6

Press the tiles firmly into place without sliding them, inserting plastic spacers (to leave space for the grout) if necessary (below). Wipe off any adhesive on the surface of the tiles with a damp sponge as you go. Continue until all whole tiles have been fixed, checking the levels from time to time. Remove the battens when the adhesive is dry.

7

Now fix the cut tiles. Mark the cutting line on the tile and place it on a cutting board, right side up. Score through with a tungsten carbide cutter held against a metal rule (below). Place matchsticks or a pencil, depending on the tile's thickness, underneath the scored line and press firmly on each side. If you're lucky, the tile will snap evenly. For odd shapes, you will need to make a template and copy the shape on to the tile, nibbling away with pincers and finishing with a tile file.

8

Fix cut tiles so that the smooth edge is next to the adjacent tile and the cut edge is next to the work-top or skirting.

9

When tiling is complete, leave the adhesive to harden as instructed on the packet. Waterproof adhesive takes longer to dry. Mix the grout (or buy ready-mixed) and spread it over the gaps with a sponge, pushing it in well and wiping away the excess with a clean damp sponge. Neaten with your finger or a lolly stick just before the grout sets.

Top Tip

Use pincers rather than a tile cutter to cut away a very narrow strip at the edge of a tile.

Top Tip

Use flexible sealant between the tiles and bath or basin after you grout.

10

When dry, wipe with a damp sponge to remove the last traces of grout, and polish the tiles with a soft cloth.

! BLOCKAGE

Don't rinse the sponges and cloths used for grouting under the tap. The grout residues may block the drain.

COMMON DOOR PROBLEMS

Doors can suffer from a range of different faults as a result of wear and tear, old age, lack of maintenance or improper hanging. Here are some cures for the most common problems.

1

Secure loose door frames by drilling a hole through the frame, then switch to a masonry drill bit and drill on into the masonry behind. Insert a long plastic frame plug, and screw the frame securely to the masonry.

2

Ease doors that stick in their frames at the top by chamfering the top edge slightly with a plane.

3

Cut out rot in the bottom of exterior door frames and replace it with new wood.

4

Hinge screw heads that are not driven fully into their recesses will prevent the door from closing. Replace the screws if necessary.

5

Hinges set too deep in their recesses can also stop the door from closing. Fit packing under the hinge leaf to cure the problem (see right).

6

If hinge screws work loose, remove them, drill out the screw holes and tap in a short piece of glued dowel. Make a new pilot hole and replace the screw.

7

If door bottoms stick slightly in solid floors, use abrasive paper to remove a little wood from the bottom edge of the door.

8

Where the door bottom sticks seriously, take it off its hinges and plane wood from the bottom edge.

How to fit a door

Hanging a new door can seem a complex operation, especially if the original door was a non-standard size. Buy a door in the next largest available size so that it can be cut down to fit.

1

First, saw off the elements that protect the corners of the door in transit, then try the door for fit by holding it against the frame. It is certain to need trimming on one or more edges. Get someone to help you hold it in place, if necessary supporting it on wedges.

2

Working from the frame side, mark round the edge of the frame with a pencil on to the face of the door against the frame, allowing a 2mm gap all round after trimming.

3

Saw across the bottom of the door and plane along the edges until the door fits correctly in the opening. Pass the plane a couple of extra times along the leading edge of the door to ensure it will clear the frame edge as it closes.

4

External door frames usually have a metal water bar along the sill. To prevent draughts and water ingress, it is important that the door closes up against this. Therefore you must cut a rebate (or step) along the bottom edge of the door on the face (outer) side. You will need a router and suitable cutter for this. Otherwise, use a circular saw to cut the rebate to the correct depth, or form it with a power planer or rebate plane.

5

If you are fitting the door in an old frame, mark the hinge positions on the back of the door while it is wedged in the opening with the correct clearance all round. Remove the door and transfer the marked hinge positions on to the edge of the door.

6

Cut the recesses with a chisel, holding it upright and striking it with a mallet to cut the outline of the recess. Then make a series of cuts about 6mm (¼ in) apart across the width of the recess. Turn the chisel so it is flat in the recess and pare out the waste wood.

7

Get someone to hold the door on wedges in its open position and then, with the hinge flaps positioned in their recesses, initially fit just one screw in each hinge. Close the door to see how it fits in the frame, adjusting the depth of the hinge recesses if it binds. When you are satisfied that it fits correctly, insert the rest of the fixing screws.

8

If you are fitting the door in a new frame, wedge the door in place and mark the hinge positions on both the door and the frame. Use three hinges for an external door. The highest one should be about 125mm (5in) from the top, the lowest about 200mm (8in) from the bottom and the third midway between the two.

9

Remove the door, mark out the hinge recesses on the door edge and frame, then cut the recesses as described above. The width of the recesses should be such that the knuckle (pivoting part) of the hinge protrudes from the edge of the door. Finally, screw the hinges in position as before.

Ease doors that stick in their frames at the top by chamfering the top edge slightly with a plane.

Mark and cut recesses in the door edge to take one leaf of the hinge, and screw it into place.

Finish the job by fitting a latch and handle.

How to fit door furniture

Once you have fitted a door in place you need to affix door furniture such as locks, a door knocker and letterplate to finish the job properly.

A back door needs a good quality mortise lock (ideally with at least five levers) and bolts top and bottom. A front door also needs a deadlocking cylinder rim latch or nightlatch so you can open it easily and quickly. Again, there should be bolts top and bottom and also a door chain and door viewer for complete security.

Locks come with fitting instructions and you must follow these carefully.

Mortise locks

Mortise locks (opposite right) are secure because the body of the lock is concealed within the thickness of the door. However, cutting too wide a slot for a lock can weaken the door, so buy the narrowest type available.

To fit this type you will have to mark the outline of the lock on the edge of the door and drill out the mortise slot to the depth of the lock case. Clean up the slot with a chisel and bore the door stile to take the key and spindle holes.

Rim locks

Rim locks (opposite left) screw to the surface of the door and are very easy to fit. The hardest part is drilling a large hole for the cylinder of the lock in the door stile. Use a large-diameter flat wood bit for this or drill a ring of small holes and cut out the waste with a pad saw.

Bolts

It is a good idea to fit bolts at the top and bottom of all external doors, but rather than fix surface-mounted barrel bolts, go for higher security mortise rack bolts. These comprise a cylindrical bolt enclosed in a barrel, which is fitted into a hole drilled in the edge of the door.

By inserting a splined key in the edge of the door, you can wind the bolt in and out. And because it is enclosed, the bolt is difficult to tamper with and therefore provides improved security.

Chains and viewers

If you want to fit a door chain you simply screw the device to the inside face of the door. This will prevent an intruder barging in should you open the door.

If you have solid doors, you should always combine this type of security with a door viewer to enable you to see who is at the door before you open it. All you have to do is drill a hole of about 13mm (½ in) diameter through the door at eye level and screw the two halves of the viewer together in it.

Door knocker

To fit a door knocker or door pull, you simply drill a hole centrally for the fixing bolt. You fit the knocker or pull in place from the outside and then hold it secure with a fixing nut or screw on the inside.

Letterplate

Fitting a letterplate is more tricky. Mark out a rectangular opening on the centre of the door, slightly larger than the plate flap. Drill a hole at each corner big enough for a power jigsaw blade to pass through. Cut out the rectangle of wood and clean up the sides of the opening with a large chisel.

Finally, drill a hole at each end of the opening to take the fixing bolts and screw the letterplate in place.

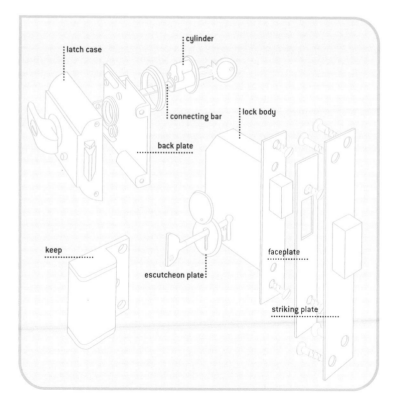

latch case · cylinder · connecting bar · lock body · back plate · keep · escutcheon plate · faceplate · striking plate

How to fit a window frame

Many homeowners choose to upgrade their windows, perhaps from wooden frames to reinforced PVC for extra security. Many nationwide companies offer this service, but there is no reason why you cannot save money and undertake the work yourself.

If your replacement frame is a conventional timber one, this will be supplied as a readymade unit that is fixed in place and then glazed on site. If it is made of plastic, aluminium or galvanised steel, this will usually be fitted into a subframe that must first be fixed into the wall opening. The new unit may well be supplied ready-glazed.

In the case of a conventional timber frame, it will probably be possible to keep the original internal window frame ledge and fit the new frame against it.

1

The new frame will probably be supplied with horns (corner projections) for protection in transit. Cut these off and give the exterior surfaces of the frame an extra coat of wood primer or preservative stain, depending on the final finish you require.

2

Lift the frame into position and check it is square – that is, with equal diagonals. Wedge it in place so that it is level and

plumb (vertical), making sure it is not under strain or twisted. If the frame is slightly too small for the opening, you can tack packing pieces on to the edge to build it out.

3

When it is correctly fitted, mark the positions of the wedges and the fixing screws. Most window frames need three or four screws on each side and these should be positioned so that they go into the middle of bricks, rather than into the mortar joints.

4

Remove the wedges and the frame and drill holes in the frame to take the fixing screws. Special zinc-plated, frame-fixing screws complete with wall plugs are available for this job.

5

Spread a layer of mortar at the bottom of the opening for the frame to rest on. Then replace the frame and the wedges, and check that everything is square.

6

Use a long masonry drill bit to make holes through the frame into the wall. Countersink these holes, then position the frame-fixing screws and plugs (there is no need to remove the frame to position the plugs) and tighten the screws so that the heads lie flush with the surface of the wood. A little wood filler will cover up the screw heads.

7

Press mortar into any wide gaps between the frame and the wall and use plaster to make good the wall on the inside of the frame. Fill any narrow gaps between the frame and the wall with mastic injected into the gap, using a trigger-operated applicator gun.

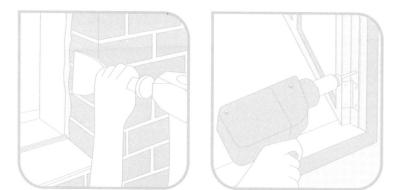

To replace a window frame, unscrew any opening casements or top lights, and carefully break out fixed panes of glass. Then saw through the frame at each corner and prise the sections away. Clean up the opening with a club hammer and cold chisel or brick bolster (above left). If no dampproof course (dpc) is present beneath the old window, lay a new dpc strip across the sill and set the new frame in position. Check that it is level, then drill holes through the sides and into the masonry so the frame can be secured with wood screws and frame plugs at each side (above right).

How to reglaze a window

Unfortunately, accidents do happen. Whether a bird has flown into a window by mistake or your children have got carried away with their game of football, there will come a time when one of your windows gets broken and the glass needs to be replaced. Although the job should be undertaken with great care (broken glass is dangerous), it is nevertheless a fairly routine job.

1

Before glazing a window, you must first treat the frame with a suitable primer paint and allow this to dry.

2

Work the putty in the hands to soften it before applying a 3–4mm thick band into the rebate of the frame. Press it out between the thumb and forefinger. If the putty is too sticky to handle easily, wrap it in newspaper for 24 hours to dry out the oil a little.

3

Now lift the glass into place in the rebate and carefully press it (edges only) back on to the putty. Hold the glass in place by inserting glazing sprigs (small wedge-shaped nails) about 200mm (8in) apart round the perimeter in front of the glass. Tap in the sprigs carefully with the edge of the glazing knife or large chisel held flat over the face of the glass.

4

Apply a second layer of putty to the outside of the glass and smooth it off to a bevel of 45 degrees with a putty knife. If the knife sticks, moisten it with water.

5

Remove excess putty from the inside and outside of the pane with the knife and allow the putty to harden for about two weeks before priming and painting it.

Gaskets

Modern double-glazed windows have gaskets to hold the glass in position. If they are not already glazed, fitting instructions will be supplied with the frames.

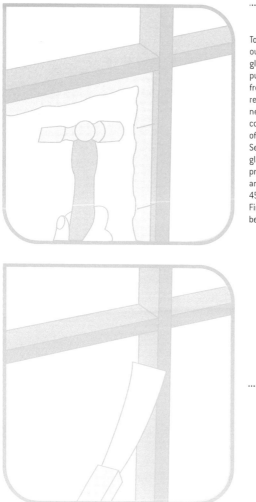

To reglaze a window, lift out the broken pieces of glass and chip out the old putty. Then press some fresh putty round the rebate and press the new pane into place to compress it to a thickness of about 3mm (⅛in). Secure the pane with glazing sprigs (left), press in the facing putty and finish it to a neat 45-degree angle all round. Finally, trim off excess bedding putty (below).

How to lift and replace floorboards

Sometimes floorboards need to be lifted to access heating pipes and electrical wiring that sit underneath; at other times the floorboard simply needs replacing because it is old or damaged. Follow these instructions to learn how to lift and replace your floorboards.

The type of floorboard determines the way each board can be lifted. If you do not know what kind you have, look for a board that has been screwed down and remove it. Alternatively, stick a knife blade between several boards. If it goes right down, the boards are square-edged. If it cannot be inserted, the boards are tongued-and-grooved.

Square-edged boards

To lift a square-edged board, you can sometimes insert a bolster chisel near one end and lever the nails free from the joists below. Insert another bolster or lever on the opposite side and work them along until the nails at each joist have been released and the board is free. Alternatively, slide a metal bar or piece of wood under the board and press down on the end to 'spring' the nails free.

If you can't get a bolster below the board, drill a 10mm (²/₅in) diameter hole near to a joist end. The nail positions will

guide you. Then cut through the board at a right-angle using a jigsaw or a pad saw, taking care not to cut any cables below. You can now raise the board as described earlier.

Tongued-and-grooved

Removing the first tongued-and-grooved board is more tricky. After that, the others are easy. First you will have to cut through the tongue along the length of the board using a circular saw or a floorboard saw. The circular saw should be set to cut to a depth of only about 12mm (½in).

Chipboard flooring

To take up a damaged area of chipboard floor you need a circular saw set to cut to a depth of either 19 or 22mm (¾ or ⅞in) depending on the thickness of the board. Make a cut along the joint between adjacent boards and lever up the board with a bolster chisel.

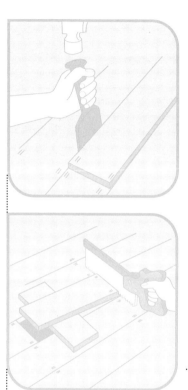

! FLOORBOARD
● FAULTS

Old boarded floors suffer from a variety of faults. Board ends may warp and lift, especially if they have been prised up before for maintenance work on services that run beneath them. Shrinkage can lead to gaps between boards or along skirting boards, while physical damage can cause splits and cracks. Boards may also bow upwards along their length, pulling up their fixings and causing the boards to creak when stepped on.

To lift old floorboards for repair or replacement, or to gain access to services run beneath them, prise up a board end with a bolster and then lever it up along its length (top). If the boards are tongued-and-grooved, saw through the tongues along each side of the board first with a circular saw set to a cutting depth of about 12mm (½in). To lift just a section of board, drill a starter hole through it beside a joist and cut across the board with a padsaw. Wedge up the cut end and saw through the board at the next joist position (bottom). Fix battens to the joist sides to support the ends of the new length of board, and nail it into place.

How to lay wooden sheet flooring

Floorboards are not the only option for the householder when laying wooden flooring. You might prefer to lay chipboard or tongued-and-grooved sheets directly on the ceiling joists. Here's how to do it.

Squared-edged flooring

Lay square-edged chipboard flooring with the long sheet edges running parallel to the joists and butt-jointed along the joist centres. Add noggings between the joists to support the short board edges, positioning them so that both boards can be nailed to each individual nogging.

Tongued-and-grooved

Lay tongued-and-grooved sheets with their long edges at right angles to the joist direction, with butt joints between the short board edges centred over a joist. Nail the boards to every joist. Stagger the joints in alternate rows of boards.

When laying square-edged flooring, nail the boards to the noggings.

How to treat rough floorboards

If boards are warped, but the trouble is only slight, you can use an electric industrial floor sander to smooth off the surface. Remove any carpet tacks and punch all nails below the surface using a nail punch and hammer, so that they do not tear the abrasive belt fitted to the sander.

A floor sander can be obtained from a tool hire shop. The sander will be supplied with sheets of abrasive, which you fit to the large revolving drum of the machine. Assuming that the boards are in an average state, then start sanding with a medium-grade abrasive and end with a fine grade to get a smoother finish. Since a large floor sander will not reach into the edges, you will also need a belt sander to finish off at the skirtings.

Because sanding is very dusty work, make sure you seal off the room, cover any furniture left in and wear a dust mask.

Sanding technique

Normally you sand a floor in the direction of the boards. If, however, they are in a poor condition, make the first pass at a 45-degree angle to the boards. Finish off working parallel with them (see right). Never work at right-angles to the boards, since this will tear the surface.

Tilt the sander off the floor before switching it on. (If you switch on with the sander flat on the floor or work too slowly, you can make indents in the floor surface.) Then lower it on to the boards and work it slowly backwards and forwards over a few feet. Then move to the next section of board and repeat the process, overlapping the previous sanded area by about 75mm (3in).

Before applying any final treatment such as varnish, you will have to vacuum the floor thoroughly to remove dust.

How to solve flooring problems

In some cases, it is not prudent to rip up sections of flooring and replace them. Where imperfections are slight (gaps in flooring or sunken boards) there are simpler remedies at hand.

Gaps

An odd gap between boards can be filled with mastic sealant. With a wider gap, glue a suitably sized wedge-shaped piece of wood and tap it into the gap. Then level it off with a plane.

Where there are lots of gaps, the quickest repair is to lay hardboard. You would normally do this anyway if you were laying a floorcovering on top.

Where you want to leave the boards exposed so they can be varnished and rugs or a carpet square laid in strategic areas, you will have to relay them. This gives you the opportunity to refix the boards upside down to provide a fresh, clean surface, although you are likely to have to do some localised sanding to remove the joist marks from the boards.

Treating sunken boards

If any of the floorboards have dropped, take them up and insert packing pieces of hardboard or plywood where they are fixed to the joists. If they have warped downwards slightly, refix them upside down and sand them smooth. If either

problem cannot be cured using these methods, then fit a replacement board of the required thickness.

Relaying boards

If you are replacing boards, lay four or five in position on the joists, butting up their edges closely. Next, nail a length of 100 x 25mm (4 x 1in) timber about 75 or 100mm (3 or 4in) away. Cut two tapered wedges and hammer them into the gap between the piece of wood and the boards. This will force the boards tightly together so that they can be nailed correctly in place. Then remove the wedges.

Repeat this with the next group of boards and carry on with this procedure until the floor is complete. You will probably have to cut a narrow strip of board to finish off at the skirting when you reach the far side of the room.

If all the boards have shrunk to leave wide gaps, it is best to lift them all and re-lay them to close up the gaps. Loose-lay four or five boards, then nail another board to the joists about 50mm (2in) away and use a floorboard cramp or a pair of wedges as shown to tighten up the first group of boards. Nail them down, remove the odd board and lay the next group in the same way. At the far side of the room, lay the last board tight against the wall and fit a cut-down strip of board in the gap.

How to lay flooring tiles

There are several types of soft floorcoverings that come in tile form. These include: carpet tiles, cork tiles, vinyl tiles and rubber tiles. There are various methods for laying these tiles: some are self-adhesive, some are laid loose and some are laid on a bed of adhesive. They all require a sound, dry, clean, level surface.

Setting out the floor

Whether the tiles are laid loose or stuck down, the procedure for marking out the floor is the same.

First, find the centre point of the floor. Do this by finding the centre point on each of the walls, measuring straight along and ignoring bay windows and doors. Take two lengths of string, coat them with chalk and pin them from one wall to the opposite. The two strings will cross in the middle of the floor at right angles to each other; the centre of the cross is the exact centre of the room. Snap each string against the floor to leave a chalk line, then remove the strings. Leave the pins for the time being.

Set out a row of tiles dry from the centre point to one wall. See what size border will have to be cut. Continue the line of tiles to the opposite wall to see the width of border on that side of the room. Move the tiles a little either way to even up the borders – aim for a margin no less than half a tile wide – and/or if it will

avoid some awkward trimming. Move the pins on each wall to the same distance.

Do the same with a row of tiles between the other two walls. Again, slight adjustments to give symmetrical, substantial borders may be necessary. Move the pins to compensate.

Remove the dry tiles, refit the strings and chalk two fresh lines. The cross will mark where the first tiles are to be laid.

Loose-laid tiles

Carpet tiles are laid loose. Most have a non-slip back but may require spots of latex adhesive if slipping is a problem.

Self-adhesive tiles

Self-adhesive tiles are laid out like other soft floor tiles. Peel off the backing and press each tile into place. Fit all the full tiles first and fill in round the walls at the end. Check the pattern match between the tiles, turning each one before sticking it to judge the best way.

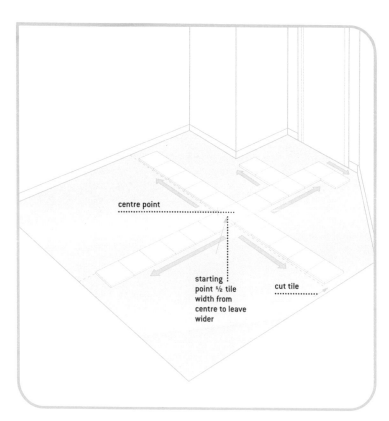

centre point

starting point ½ tile width from centre to leave wider

cut tile

Above: When laying floor tiles it is important to dry-lay a few strategic tiles to find out where cut tiles will be and to adjust their widths to give a balanced look to the final job. Starting from the measured centre point of the floor, work outwards in a cross shape in the direction of the arrows and adjust the starting point as needed.

Left: Peeling the paper backing off a self-adhesive tile; arrows may be printed on the back to indicate the direction of laying.

How to lay carpet

Most householders spend an extra few pounds getting the contractor who supplied their carpet to fit it. However, knowing how to fit a carpet does come in useful when you've moved house and you have old but perfectly good carpets to be re-used, or perhaps you'd risk laying a cheaper quality carpet yourself.

The carpet must, of course, be larger than the room for which it's intended. It may be entirely the wrong shape and necessitate a lot of trimming. Lay it down to 75mm (3in) larger than needed all round. This will make fitting more manageable.

The carpet should be arranged so that the pile faces towards the door and away from the main source of light. If a join must be made, try to avoid the area of heaviest traffic and always make the join along the traffic area rather than across it. Where a join is used to make up the width of a room, it should be on the side away from the door. Do not attempt to lay carpet on an uneven floor: the edges of boards will soon rub away at the underlay or woven backing and will create lines in the carpet. Nail down loose boards, turn warped ones or plane down the edges against the grain and fill any large cracks.

Foam-backed carpet

This is much easier to lay than the woven variety: it needs no underlay, no stretching and no gripper rods or tacks. It's stuck to the floor around the perimeter of the room with double-sided tape. To prevent the foam backing sticking to the floorboards under friction, and tearing away when the carpet is lifted, a paper lining is arranged over the boards. Special paper can be bought or strong brown paper can be used.

Firstly, cover the floor to within 50mm (2in) of the wall with the paper underlay. Join it if necessary with single-sided adhesive tape and fix it round the edges with double-sided tape. Stick lengths of double-sided adhesive tape all round the room.

Spread out the carpet on the floor so that it laps up to the skirting all around. Roughly trim off the excess carpet. Peel the back of the double-sided tape and smooth the carpet down on to it.

Woven carpet

There are two ways to lay woven carpet: by tacking or with tackless fittings. Always buy new underlay when fitting a new carpet. A knee-kicker, which can be hired, is essential for stretching the carpet into place.

The fittings, or gripper strips, are thin wood laths with barbs, which are nailed in a continuous line around the room. Position the underlay right up to the inside edge of the gripper rods and fix it to the floor.

The carpet has to be stretched over the gripper rods to be held firm and flat by the barbs. First roll out the carpet and trim the excess, leaving about 50mm (2in) of overlap. Use the knee-kicker to stretch the carpet between corners, fixing as you go.

Fitting around pipes

You'll probably have to cut the carpet to fit around central heating and plumbing pipes emerging from the floor. To do this, fit the carpet up to the wall on which the pipe is located, then make an incision in the edge parallel with the centre of the pipe; measure from the skirting to the pipe, then cut out a small circle of carpet this distance from its edge.

Top: Peeling off the backing strip of the double-sided tape before pressing the carpet on to it; keep the carpet taut as you proceed.

Bottom: Using a knee-kicker to stretch the carpet on to the grippers; adjust the teeth to grip the woven backing, press down and knee-kick the pad.

How to level a solid floor

Solid, level floors are required as a base on which to mount tiles. You can use this method to lay a whole floor or to fill in gaps and inconsistencies in an existing solid floor.

Using screed

You can fill irregularities on a solid floor with cement mortar and then smooth it over, up to about 3mm (¹⁄₁₀in) deep, with a self-smoothing screed. This is mixed with water to form a creamy paste, which you pour on to the floor and roughly spread out with a steel float. The screed will automatically smooth out any trowel marks before it hardens. This takes up to 12 hours to harden completely, but can be walked on after four hours.

READY MIX

With irregularities up to about 9mm (¹⁄₃in) deep, you can apply a ready-mixed screed to fill in and level the surface.

CEMENT MORTAR

Indentations up to 50mm (2in) deep can be filled by resurfacing the floor with a conventional cement mortar screed consisting of three parts sharp sand to one part cement. Before applying the screed, paint the floor surface with PVA bonding agent to improve adhesion.

Trowel the cement out evenly and leave it to find its own level and harden.

How to fit skirting boards

Over the years the skirting boards can take quite a hammering from being knocked by vacuum cleaners, furniture legs and so on. In fact, that's what they're there for – to protect the plaster of the wall, which would soon fall apart under this treatment. Eventually, the skirtings will become scruffy and you will want to repair small sections or even replace complete lengths.

Removing skirting

In most cases, the skirtings will be nailed in place, which makes removal and replacement easy. However, always make a check for screws first and release any you find from the affected area.

Remove entire lengths of skirting by prising them from the wall with a bolster chisel and wooden wedges, starting at an external corner or where the skirting meets a door frame architrave. If the skirting runs between two internal corners, you may have to cut through it to pull it away as its ends may be trapped behind the ends of the abutting skirtings.

Replacing skirting

To replace just a section of skirting, drive a bolster chisel down behind it to prise it from the wall, then drive in wooden wedges on each side of the damage. Cut out the damaged piece with a saw, making the cuts slope inwards at an angle.

Cut a new piece of board to fit the gap, sloping the ends to match the cuts in the original board. If necessary, nail wooden spacer blocks to the wall so that they just fit under the cut ends of the original board. Use masonry nails if fixing to brickwork. Drive the nail heads down with a punch and fill the holes before painting.

How to fit a handrail

There are various problems that can affect staircases, from creaking treads to loose or missing balusters. Follow this advice to learn how to repair or fit a handrail.

Repairing handrails

Handrails with balusters usually have their ends tenoned into the newel posts (the main upright stems of a staircase). If an end becomes loose, simply secure it by driving a screw or dowel peg in through the side of the newel post into the handrail tenon.

Where a handrail is damaged, cut out the offending section and replace it with a new matching piece, if available. Saw at a sloping angle to the line of the rail to give a greater contact area for the new piece to form a scarf-joint. Glue and screw the piece into place. On the underside of the rail, screw on a metal plate as reinforcement. Then refix the baluster tops (page 84).

If a matching section of handrail is not available, then you can either have a piece specially machined or else replace the complete rail with a different one.

Refixing a wall-mounted handrail

Wider staircases and those having a wall either side should have a handrail fixed to a wall to provide any necessary support for those who need it while using the stairs.

The only fault likely here is if the screw fixings become loose. Sometimes the handrail is supported on brackets that are screwed to the wall. Depending on its type, you might be able to detach a single bracket for refixing or, possibly, you will have to remove the complete handrail to remake the fixings.

Either way, you need to refix the screws after plugging the old holes with filler and drilling new ones. Insert wall plugs and screws the same size as the old ones to make the bracket secure.

If the rail is screwed directly to the wall, it may be possible to replace the existing (loose) screw with a thicker one -- even though this may mean drilling a new hole through the rail. If this does not work, then take the rail down completely and make a similar repair to that previously described.

To ensure all the screw holes line up again, replace the rail while you mark off the position of the new hole. Remove the rail, drill and plug the hole and then replace and refix the rail. This is the only way you can be sure the holes will line up. Where you are fitting a new handrail or replacing an old one, the important thing to remember is that it must run parallel with the string throughout its length. If it does not, it will prove very awkward and disorientating for anyone using it.

Mark the position for the rail on the wall at the top of the stairs, then screw it to the wall. Repeat this at the bottom. When you are satisfied with its position, mark the intermediate holes and then remove the rail while you drill and plug the wall. If you are using brackets, fix these to the rail first before screwing the whole assembly to the wall.

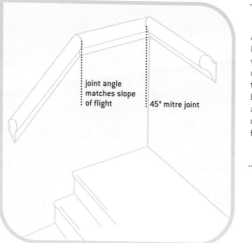

joint angle matches slope of flight

45° mitre joint

An inner handrail may be secured directly to the wall beside the flight, or may be mounted clear of the wall on handrail brackets. The rail follows any change of slope or direction taken by the flight itself.

How to fit balusters

Most traditional staircases feature balusters – wooden splints that run vertically from the handrail to the stair. Some homeowners find it a daunting prospect to repair or replace damaged balusters because of the poor accessibility of the baluster. This is how to do it.

Cut and closed string

Balusters vary depending on the type of staircase. Balusters on cut string staircases fit into mortises or slots in the ends of the treads. On a closed string staircase, they rest in a groove in the string capping and have short lengths of timbers set between them as spacers. Their top ends are either skew-nailed to the handrail or set in a groove in its underside.

Single replacements

Replacing a missing baluster normally means having to dismantle the balustrade. However, it is possible to replace the odd one by splicing a new baluster into two at an angle in a convenient position, fitting new top and bottom pieces into the rail and string and then carefully remarrying the mating halves with glue and countersunk screws.

Preparation

If you have to replace several balusters, then make sure that identical ones are available before completely dismantling the staircase. Square-section balusters are easy to match, but turned balusters may have to be specially made. If you give an undamaged baluster to a skilled woodturner, he will be able to make replicas but it will be expensive.

Fitting

If the balusters on a cut-string staircase have worked loose, drive small glue-soaked timber wedges into any gaps in the tread mortise. Then, to secure them completely, drive in two nails or fine screws at an angle to lock the end of the baluster to the tread. With closed-string flights, skew-nail the baluster to the string.

With either type, do the same at the point where the baluster meets the handrail. Finish off by concealing the repair using wood filler.

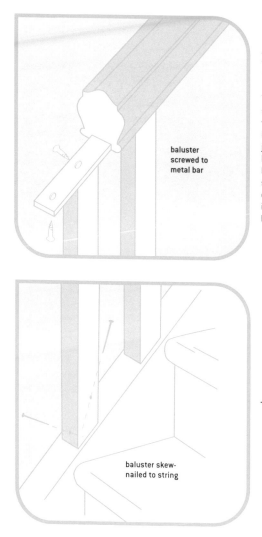

baluster
screwed to
metal bar

baluster skew-
nailed to string

A variety of carpentry techniques and specialist fittings are used to assemble the balustrade. The handrail itself may be secured to the newel post with brackets, and lengths of rail are often joined with concealed handrail bolts. The balusters may be simply skew-nailed into place, or may be set in mortises in the handrail and housings in the treads.

How to fix creaking treads

Creaky treads on a staircase are certainly not a serious issue for the homeowner – burst water pipes, for instance, will cause you much greater concern. However, like a poorly oiled door hinge, it is one of those annoying gripes. Fortunately, a solution is at hand.

The problem of creaking treads is caused by staircase timbers shrinking, which allows adjacent parts to rub together when someone uses the stairs. The situation has tended to be increasingly common where central heating has been introduced.

Access from below

If the underside of the staircase is accessible via a cupboard, the first things to look for are the wedges securing the ends of the treads and risers into their grooves in the strings.

If these are loose, tap them in firmly with a mallet. If they will not tap in, then remove them, coat them with woodworking adhesive and hammer them back into place. It is rare to find one missing, but if you do it is very easy to cut and fit a replacement.

If that does not cure the problem, fix the back of each creaky tread to the bottom of the riser above it using two screws, placed one-third and two-thirds of the way across. The screws will need to be 50mm (2in) long. To avoid splitting the wood, first drill pilot holes up through the rear edge of the tread into the centre of the riser. Countersink the screw heads.

Finally, secure the joint between the front of each tread and the top edge of the riser beneath it by gluing and screwing wooden blocks into the angle between them. Use two blocks to each tread.

Access from above

If there is no access, tackle the problem from above. Use recessed repair brackets to secure the treads to the risers. Screw the front of each creaky tread to the top edge of the riser beneath by driving screws down through the tread nosing. Use two screws and countersink the heads neatly so that they will not snag the carpet underlay or backing when this is replaced.

At the rear of each tread, prise open the joint between the tread and the riser above, using a chisel, and squirt in pva woodworking adhesive right along the gap. If possible, do the job last thing at night, when the stairs are less likely to be used until the adhesive has set.

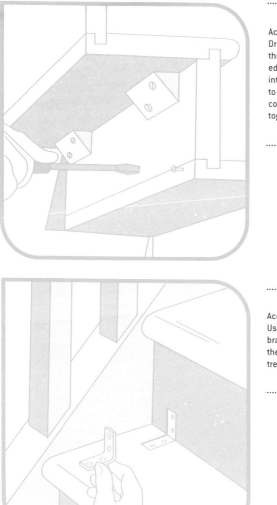

Access from below:
Drive screws
through the rear
edge of each riser
into the tread
to lock the two
components
together.

Access from above:
Use recessed repair
brackets to secure
the rear edges of the
treads to the risers.

How to lay stair carpet

Because of the frequent changes in elevation, it is harder to lay carpet stairs, than, say, your hallway. But don't let that put you off. If you have successfully carpeted other rooms, then why not the stairs?

Stairs can be carpeted with fitted carpet, or what's called a runner – a strip.

Fitting a runner

This is the easier of the two methods. A woven carpet runner also allows the carpet to be moved from time to time to equalise wear. Old-fashioned stair rods with side clips can be used to hold a runner in place and form part of the stair décor, but it is now more usual to use gripper strips. Special pinless grippers are available for use with foam-backed carpets; the carpet is held in tight jaws. The wooden strips are used in pairs, one at the back of the tread, one at the bottom of the riser, or you can buy a metal version that's already formed into a right angle.

Cut the strips to length, if necessary, 38mm (1½in) shorter than the width of the carpet using tinsnips or secateurs for wooden strips, a hacksaw for the metal type. Nail them into place, omitting the bottom riser. The gap between each pair of wooden strips should be just big enough to squeeze the carpet down into.

Cut the underlay to fit between the rods and tack close to the rods, omitting the bottom tread. No underlay is needed with foam-backed carpet.

FITTING THE BOTTOM STEP

With a runner, an extra length of carpet is included so that it can be moved up to even out the wear taken on the treads; this is folded underneath the bottom step. The pile should run down the stairs to prevent uneven shading and promote longer wear.

Start at the bottom of the stairs. Tack the end of the carpet face downwards to the bottom tread, at the back, close to the gripper. Run it down over the tread to the bottom of the last riser, fold it back and tack the fold to the riser and tread. Run the carpet up the stairs, stretching it over the gripper rods and pushing it down between them with a bolster. It should join landing carpet at the top of the last riser. If there is no carpet on the landing take the stair runner over the top of the final riser, turn under the edge and tack down.

Fitting stair carpet

The fixings for a fitted stair carpet are as for a runner. The extra length of woven carpet is not needed at the bottom, though, and underlay should be fitted to all the steps. The gripper rods should be the full width of the stairs (right). Fit the carpet from the top of the flight. The landing carpet should overlap on to the stairs and down to the bottom of the uppermost riser. The stair carpet must be stretched over the gripper rods as usual and pushed down between them. In addition, it will have to be trimmed to fit at the edges. No fixings are needed at the edges.

FITTING ON WINDING STAIRS

Where the stairs go round a bend, gripper rods cannot be used in the usual way. The carpet can be cut or folded to fit the turn.

Woven carpet Fit the gripper rods only to the treads on winding stairs. Fold the surplus carpet, with the fold falling downwards, and tack it to the bottom of the riser at 75mm (3in) intervals. Stretch the carpet over the next rod up and repeat the folding and tracking process.

Foam-backed Omit the pinless rods altogether on winding stairs. Tack the carpet to the tread, right at the back so that the tacks are not too noticeable. Fold down the surplus and tack neatly at the bottom of the riser.

Tacking gripper strips to the back of the tread and the bottom of the riser, leaving a gap into which the carpet can be pushed.

Cutting off surplus carpet on a winder; cover each tread separately, cutting off along the crease at the gripper strips.

How to remove a fireplace

If you have fireplaces in the house and decide to remove any or all of them, you will have to take away the surround and seal up the opening. This is not a particularly difficult job to carry out, but it may involve a considerable amount of work and mess.

Fire surrounds are usually screwed or nailed to the wall through metal lugs or wire loops attached to the surround on each side, close to the top. The lugs will have been plastered over. So first chip away the plaster to expose them.

When you have located the fixings, you may be able to saw the heads off the securing screws. It is most unlikely that you will be able to undo the screws; however, it may be possible to cut them off with a chisel and a club hammer.

With someone to help steady the surround, which will be very heavy, the hearth can be prised from the floor. A garden spade is ideal for this. Have some timber wedges handy to slip under it to enable you to get a handhold underneath. As you drag the hearth out of the way, you will find the concrete constructional hearth, which should be retained.

Timber surrounds

A timber surround may have a tiled or cast-iron insert. The timber itself will be a hollow box section fixed to battens nailed or screwed to the wall. The surround will

probably be fixed to the battens by screws. It may, however, be difficult to find these screws since the heads will be covered with filler. A metal cable and pipe detector may help locate them. Carefully chip away the filler, enabling you to remove the screws. Keep the surround in good condition.

The tiled or cast-iron insert will probably be held by lugs fitted at the top and sides. These will be visible when the outer timber surround is removed.

Cast-iron surrounds

Cast-iron fire surrounds are definitely valuable – and fragile. So take great care when removing them. They will be held by metal lugs set in the wall plaster at each side of the surround, close to the top and just under the mantelshelf. Because the lugs can crack off, drill through the fixing screw heads to remove them. There may also be lugs along the top edge of the mantelshelf, so check before removing the surround.

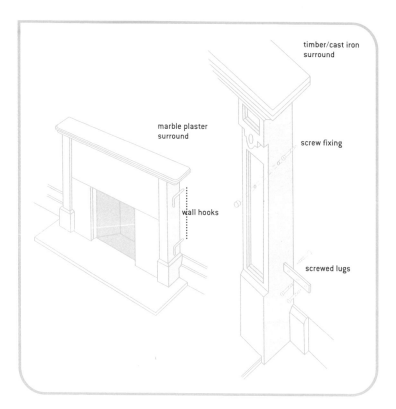

marble plaster
surround

timber/cast iron
surround

screw fixing

wall hooks

screwed lugs

! **THINK TWICE**

Timber and cast-iron fire surrounds
could be valuable, so think twice
before removing them. They could
also be in keeping with the style of
the property and perhaps be worth
more than the fireplace you are
thinking of installing.

Fire surrounds may be
secured to the wall in
a variety of ways – by
wall ties, lugs, dowels
or screws and plugs. The
fixings are generally at
either side of the fire
surround, concealed
beneath the wall plaster.

TIP 44

How to replace a fireback

Removing a fireback is a messy job, so empty the room as far as possible and cover any remaining items with dust sheets. Wear old clothes and a dust mask and lay extra dust sheets over the hearth and the floor around the fireplace. Take away any separate parts of the fire such as the grate and then remove the fireback in pieces, using a cold chisel and hammer to break it up.

There may be a fire-resistant rope between the fireback and the back of the surround. It will probably be asbestos-based and should be left in place if it is in good condition. If the rope is crumbling, however, you will have to remove it – but very carefully.

1

Wearing a dust mask and gloves, first lay plastic sheets in the opening, then spray the rope with water to dampen it. Place it in a plastic bag for disposal by the local authority. The plastic sheets should also be disposed of in a similar way.

2

Behind the fireback will be loose cement and rubble. If this is in sound condition, it can be left. If, however, the heat has made it crumble badly, you should shovel it up and clear the cavity, which is known as the builder's opening. This is, incidentally, a good stage of the job at which to have the chimney flue swept clean.

3

The fireback may be supplied in one or two pieces. A one-piece fireback will be cast with a central horizontal cutting line. If you tap the back gently along this line with a bolster chisel and hammer, the two halves will separate.

4

Put the bottom half of the fireback in position so that it lightly compresses the fire-resistant rope at the back of the surround. If this has been removed, put a straight piece of wood across the opening to be sure that the front face of the fireback will be just behind the inside edge of the surround when it is fitted.

5

Mark the outline of the fireback on the hearth, remove the fireback, dampen the hearth and spread a layer of fire cement on it. Lift the fireback into place and tap it down until it is correctly positioned and level.

6

Now place two thicknesses of corrugated cardboard behind the fireback to provide an expansion gap between that and the infilling that has to be put into the builder's opening.

7

Fill in behind the fireback with vermiculite mortar – made from one part hydrated lime or cement and four parts vermiculite (as used for loft insulation). Alternatively, make up a mix of one part lime, two parts soft sand and four parts broken brick. These soft insulated fillings will allow the fireback to expand under heat without cracking. They will also absorb heat to protect the builder's opening.

Remove the existing fireback with a hammer and chisel.

8

Lay a bed of fire cement on the top edge of the lower section of the fireback, lift the top section into place and tap it down. Again, put two layers of corrugated cardboard behind the fireback and fill in with weak insulating mortar. Tamp down the filling with a stick and, at the top, smooth it off at an angle of about 45 degrees to form a smooth 'throat' into the flue. Sloping mortar may also be needed at the sides to prevent the formation of any ledges, where soot could otherwise collect.

Trowel fire cement along the top edge of the lower fireback section.

How to block up a fireplace

There are basically two ways to seal a fireplace opening – by fitting plasterboard over a timber frame or by building a brick or block wall and plastering over it in the normal way.

In both cases it is important to leave an opening for ventilation. By providing a gentle flow of air through the flue, you will prevent the chimney from becoming damp. Before starting any work, make sure you have the chimney swept.

Timber frame

The timber frame method is best if you are likely to want to open up the fireplace at a later date or if you are sealing the opening for use with a gas fire. In this case, the cover should be of asbestos-free insulation board, rather than ordinary plasterboard.

Bricking-up

Bricking-up produces a solid wall that is unlikely to crack. Of course, you could always remove the bricks later on, but they will not prove as easy to dislodge as a plasterboard infill on a timber frame.

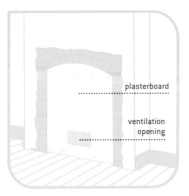

plasterboard

ventilation opening

brick or blockwork

ventilation opening

How to open up a fireplace

There are very few rooms that don't look better when a previously filled chimney breast is opened and the fireplace restored. The fireplace is the natural focal point of the room and the decorative impact it makes is well worth the sacrifice of wall space, even in quite small rooms.

YOU WILL NEED

Candle

Hammer

Bolster, or pointing chisel

Before you begin, look around for fireplaces that suit the style of your house. If you want an unusual design or one in a very small size, you may do best to look for authentic period pieces from specialists or architectural salvage firms. Alternatively, as grates and mantelpieces in good condition and at a reasonable price can be difficult to find, you may find it easier to settle for a reproduction fireplace.

1

Locate the chimney breast. It may be covered by hardboard or plasterboard, which are simple to remove, or it may be bricked in.

2

If the fireplace has been closed properly, you'll find an airbrick set into the wall to prevent damp. Insert a large chisel into the mortar surrounding it, and tap it with a hammer. Remove the airbrick carefully. If the fireplace has been filled with bricks and there is no airbrick, take out a few bricks about 300mm (12in) from the floor.

3

Light a candle and place it in the fireplace. If the flame is drawn upwards, the chimney is clear. If it goes out, ask a builder for advice.

4

If the chimney is clear, unblock the opening, taking care not to damage the lintel across the top of the fireplace.

5

Clean out the original fireplace and check that the fireback is usable and not cracked, replacing it if necessary before you fit the new fireplace.

Household
Fittings

Fixtures and fittings are an essential part of any household renovation project. When moving in to your last property, did you struggle to fit the curtain poles? Perhaps you find it difficult to erect bookshelves that are both sturdy and level, or maybe you are always troubled by the intricacies of assembling flat-pack furniture. This chapter will transform your capabilities in all these areas of home improvement.

How to put up a shelf

Shelves are the most flexible form of storage. Once you can put up a shelf, you'll have mastered the basic techniques needed for hanging everything from paintings and mirrors to wall cupboards. It's easy when you know how, as long as you make sure the shelf is absolutely level and choose suitable wall fixings so that the brackets are secure.

YOU WILL NEED

Bradawl

Pencil

Power drill

Screwdriver

Shelves, brackets and fixings (including wall plugs if necessary)

Spirit level

1

Plan the distance between the shelves. Make sure they're broad enough and far apart enough for your needs. The heavier the load, the more supports you will need. Make sure brackets are a minimum of 400mm (16in) apart for bookshelves or when fitting glass shelves.

2

Check that the screws are the right size for the brackets and long enough to take the weight, and that the wall plugs and drill bit size are compatible. 'Universal' wall plugs cover a range of common screw sizes.

3

Mark a line along the wall where the shelf will be, using a spirit level to check that it's straight. Hold the brackets in place and mark the screw holes (opposite, top), before checking the horizontal with a spirit level once more.

4

With a solid wall, use a masonry drill bit to make holes for the first bracket, about 40mm (1½in) deep where marked (opposite, centre). Work slowly to make sure the drill doesn't overheat.

To mark the drilling depth, twist a piece of Sellotape around the drill bit marking off the first 40mm (1½in).

For breeze block or hollow plasterboard walls, use an ordinary drill bit the correct size for the fixing. When working on wood, use a bradawl to start the screw holes as that will stop the timber splitting.

5

Push in the wall plugs until they are flush with the surface, and loosely screw the bracket into place, keeping a check that it is vertical with a spirit level.

6

Repeat with the furthest bracket, and check both vertical and horizontal levels. Repeat until all the brackets are in place, carefully checking the levels each time, and making any adjustments necessary.

To avoid making unnecessary holes in the wall, drill and screw just one hole for each bracket, marking the others in pencil until you are sure the shelf will be level (bottom right).

7

Screw the brackets firmly in place on the wall and put up the shelf. Mark the position of the small retaining screws that secure the shelf to the bracket. Remove the shelf and make small 'pilot' holes in it with a bradawl before replacing the shelf on the brackets and screwing into place manually.

How to assemble flat-pack furniture

Whether you are putting together a simple bookshelf, a small bathroom cabinet or a more complex piece of flat-pack furniture, such as a computer desk with a sliding shelf, follow these steps to success.

Never use a knife to slit open the packaging, as you could damage the panels inside. Lay the pack flat and release the staples, tape or other fixings one by one. Then you can lift out the panels individually, stack them up neatly and retrieve any small bags of fixing devices that may be concealed within the packaging.

1

Unpack the kit and lay out all the components, including the assembly fittings and any other items of hardware such as hinges, handles and feet (opposite, top left).

2

Identify all the parts and check that you have the right number of fixings – there is usually a checklist included with the instructions. If any appear to be missing, look again inside the packaging. If you still cannot locate the missing pieces, return the complete unit to the store and ask for a replacement.

3

Start with the base panel, adding any fixed feet first of all. Build tall units, such as bookshelves or wardrobes, on their backs to make the assembly manageable. If the unit has castors or wheels, fit these last or the unit will keep moving about as you try to assemble it.

4

Connect the first side panel to the base panel. The simplest units have pre-drilled holes through which you can drive screws supplied with the furniture. Many units use a combination of glued dowels and cam fixings. In this case, place the dowels and screwed pegs in the base unit and then offer up the side panel. Glue and locate all the dowels in the side panel, then tighten the fixings.

5

Connect the second side panel to make a three-sided box. If the unit has a back panel, locate this in the grooves in the side panels and slide it into place. Then finish the box by fixing the top panel in position.

6

Many fixings come with cover discs that match the colour of the wood or veneer of the finished item. These make a tidy job of disguising the fixings once the furniture is complete. They can be prised out of their holes if you need access to the fixings to dismantle the furniture.

7

Follow the instructions with the unit to add any doors. They will be hung on some form of spring-loaded hinges, and the fitting and fixing holes will all be pre-drilled in the doors and cabinet sides. Fit the hinge body to the door and the mounting plate to the cabinet sides, then connect the two with the short machine screws and adjust them so they hang squarely.

8

Add any shelves, door handles and other internal or external fittings. Double-check that all the assembly fittings are tight, and that you do not have any parts left over. Finally, fit wheels or castors if these are part of the kit.

! KEY TO SUCCESS

When you have finished putting a piece of furniture together, tape the assembly key and instructions securely to the back, so that you will always have them handy if you need to move, dismantle or adjust your furniture.

How to box in pipes

Some people regard visible pipes in the home as an eyesore, but with a little time and minimal woodworking skills they can be hidden from view.

1

Measure the distance that the pipes protrude from the wall, making an allowance for any clips, brackets or fittings such as valves. Make the side panels slightly wider than this measurement.

2

If the panels are narrow, you may be able to drive the screws through their edges – mark the positions with a pencil. If not, fix anchor plates flush with the back edges of the panels.

3

Attach the side panels, screwing them firmly into position. If screwing to a plywood panel, you may need to make pilot holes; in masonry, you need to drill and plug the holes.

4

Cut the front panel of the box from 6mm (¼ in) plywood, using a jigsaw or circular saw. Offer it up and check the fit. If the panel does not need to be removed again, it can be nailed in place.

5

If the panel needs to be removable, drill screw holes and secure it with 19mm (¼ in) screws. Cup washers under the screw heads will protect the panel if it is likely to be removed often.

6

Trim the edges of the front panel flush with the side panels with a block plane (below). Then drive any nail heads below the surface and fill. Sand the entire box prior to applying a finish.

How to fit a curtain pole

When moving into a new home you might sometimes find the previous owner has removed curtain poles. Alternatively, you may not like the style of pole used, preferring wood to metal, for instance. Either way, you need to know how to fix a curtain pole with the minimum of fuss.

1

Draw a guideline on the wall as for fixing brackets for a track on the wall.

2

Measure how far above the centre of the bracket the screw hole is and make the drilling marks that distance above the line, 100mm (4in) from each end, and in the centre if needed. Alternatively, if the bracket is in two parts, make drilling marks on the guideline through the holes on the mounting plate.

3

Drill and plug the holes. Drive in the screws, letting the heads project; or screw in place the plates for two-part brackets. Fit the brackets in place (right).

4

Position the pole, centring it on the brackets, and slide on the rings. Make sure that one ring is outside each end bracket and the remainder are between the brackets. Push the finials firmly into place at each end of the pole.

5

Drive the screw provided into the hole in the base of each bracket until it bites into the pole. This prevents the pole from being dislodged as you draw the curtains.

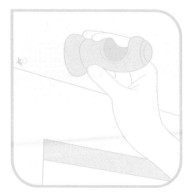

How to make a picture frame

There's no need to restrict the number of pictures you hang or let pictures and photos gather dust until you can afford professional framing. With a few simple tools and materials and basic DIY skills, you can produce excellent frames for minimum outlay. Use the following techniques for prints and inexpensive original paintings.

1

Trim the picture if necessary to remove any rough edges and pin holes.

2

Work out the external measurements of the frame by using the following formula. Measure the width of the moulding, deducting the width of the rebate (recess). Double this and add to the length and width measurements of the picture, adding an extra 3mm (¹⁄₁₀in) to the length and width to allow for clearance.

3

Make sure the mitre box is firmly fixed and clamp the moulding into place, protecting it from denting with pieces of card. It should lie flat in the mitre box, with the rebate edge underneath and facing away from you.

4

Put the saw in the slot in the mitre box, and cut the first mitre at the end of one of the lengths of moulding.

Top Tip

Practise mitring offcuts of wood until you're certain of cutting a clean edge and making sure the mitres go the right way.

5

Mark in pencil the external length of the longest side (as calculated in step 2) so you know where to cut. Cut the second mitre, angled in the opposite direction.

6

Using this length as a guide, measure and mitre the other long side.

7

Cut and mitre two pieces of moulding for the width.

8

Return the pieces of moulding to the mitre box and clamp into place to make sure they form a perfect right-angled corner (see below).

9

Place a length of moulding in the vice with the longer outer edge uppermost and drill a tiny hole near the end of the moulding, but not too close to the edges or the wood will split. Drill the hole at one end only. Repeat at one end of the other three mouldings.

10

Taking a long piece of moulding, put it in the vice and brush the cut edge of the undrilled end with glue. Place the pin-hole end of the shorter side on it to form two sides of the frame. Hammer in the pins, punch in and wipe away any glue that's squeezed out.

11

Remove the two pieces carefully and lay flat to dry. Repeat with the other side and then assemble the frame.

12

When dry, rub down with fine glass paper and stain or varnish the frame if required.

13

Cut the backing from hardboard with a hand saw, marking out the cutting lines with a pencil and set square.

14

Check that the glass and mount are clean and lay the frame face down on the table. Insert the glass into the rebate, followed by the mount, picture and hardboard. You may need to use glazing sprigs to keep it all in place if it doesn't fill the rebate, or turnclips if it all lies flush with the surface. Seal the back with masking tape.

15

Fix screw eyes or D rings to the back of the frame, one-third of the way down. Attach enough cord to come just below the top of the picture. Measure from the frame to the top of the picture wire or cord when fully stretched and mark the same point on the wall. Fix a picture hook to this point and hang the picture (below).

Outside
the Home

DIY jobs inside the home often take priority — after all it's where you spend most of your time. However, the outside of your home is at the mercy of the elements, and damage can easily occur to roofs, walls and garden fences. Whether you need to repair a leaking gutter joint or fill some cracked rendering, this chapter will tell you everything you need to know to master exterior maintenance.

How to repair a garage roof

Garage roofs can be more of a problem than conventional pitched roofs because they are mostly flat. Water can gather around dead leaves, etc, eventually rotting and penetrating the roof covering. Check your garage roof regularly for signs of any ill effects.

If you discover a leaking roof, check from the underside to see if you can trace the source of the leak during rain. This can be particularly difficult with a felt-covered flat roof, especially if the underside is lined, as it should be, with insulating material.

The problem is that rain can enter at one place and travel a considerable distance along roofing joists before it shows itself as a damp patch on the garage ceiling.

Flat roof repair

With a leak in a felt-covered flat roof, scrape away any stone chippings from the affected area. Then paint the roof with flashing strip primer, which is a bitumen-like product, and allow this to dry. The process takes a few minutes, while the primer changes from brown to black. Then stick a patch of metal-faced, self-adhesive flashing strip over the hole or crack and bed it down well.

Pitched roof repair

The same method of repair can be used for pitched roofed garages, where metal or cement-based corrugated roofing sheets have developed holes. However, this is only a temporary measure, since you should eventually change the sheets for new ones.

Adjoining garages

If the garage is attached, leaks often develop between the roof and where it joins the house wall. You may also spot the effects of differential movement between the house and the garage where the two buildings meet if the foundations were not built deep enough.

There is little you can do about this. If the building is showing no signs of cracking elsewhere, you might as well leave it. Fill any gaps with non-setting mastic and cover the joint with a self-adhesive flashing strip, which should be able to absorb the movement.

Carports

The usual roof covering for a carport is clear corrugated plastic sheeting. If this starts to leak, it is often a sign that the plastic has become brittle and is nearing the end of its useful life. So be prepared to strip the roof and fix new sheets.

In the meantime, you can extend the life of the roof by sealing any leaks with self-adhesive waterproof tape. If the damage is extensive, replace individual sheets with new ones with matching corrugations.

To repair a corrugated carport or garage roof, free the fixings securing the damaged sheet so that you can slide it out. Buy a sheet of replacement roofing to match the profile of the existing roof sheeting, and cut it to length using a jigsaw and a guide batten (top). Slide the new sheet into place, drill holes for the new fixings and secure it to the roof joists (bottom). If you suspect that the old sheeting contains asbestos, contact your local authority for guidance on its safe disposal.

How to fix roof tiles

Roof tiles repel all water from a pitched roof and direct it into the guttering of your house. Damaged tiles will almost certainly allow water into the upper recesses of your home, which will cause damp problems. Damaged tiles will also slip from their mooring, damaging other tiles on their way to the ground. So it pays to deal with damaged tiles promptly.

On the whole, tiles are easy to remove and replace, so it is not worth trying to patch them up with mastic or glass fibre paste if they have cracked or are broken. The only exception is for emergency repairs or if replacement tiles are not readily available.

Temporary repairs

To make temporary repairs, there is a simple method you can use. First, ease up the tiles in the row above the broken tile using small timber wedges. Cover the crack or missing piece of tile using self-adhesive flashing strip.

If the tiles have a sandy finish, it may be necessary to paint the surface with flashing strip primer. This is supplied with the rolls of flashing strip. Alternatively, you can use waterproof repair tape or trowel-on roofing mastic, which can be reinforced with patches of roofing felt or strips of aluminium cooking foil covered with more mastic.

Replacing tiles

Ease up the tiles in the row above the damaged or missing one, using small timber wedges. With the tip of a large builder's trowel, lift the damaged tile high enough so that the nibs at the top on the underside of the tile clear the tiling batten holding the tile in place.

In most cases, plain tiles will simply lift out. Sometimes, however, the tiles are held with nails, particularly in the case of interlocking ones. Here you must prise the tile up to pull the nails out. Hire a slate ripper for this purpose.

With the adjacent tiles still wedged up, use the builder's trowel to lift the new tile into place so that the nibs hook over the batten. When the tile is correctly positioned, you can remove the wedges so the tiles above drop back into place.

If you have to replace tiles over a large area, work up the roof slope, nailing every fourth row in the case of plain tiles and alternate rows for interlocking tiles.

To replace a missing or damaged tile, drive timber wedges in to raise the tiles above the affected area. If the damaged tile cannot be lifted out easily, release it by using a slate ripper to cut through the nails holding it to the tiling batten. Then slide a replacement tile into place and remove the wedges.

To secure loose ridge tiles, lift the tile off and chip away any old mortar. Then bed the edges of the tile on fresh mortar and point between it and its neighbours.

How to fix a roof slate

Some homeowners opt to tile their roof with slates rather than ceramic tiles – this is largely a matter of aesthetics, as both tiles and slates perform the same function of weather-proofing the roof. However, the techniques required to remove and replace a slate are different to that for a tile.

Slates are held in place with two nails driven into the batten or boarding beneath. In time, these nails corrode and the slates blow away or simply slip out of place.

If this happens over a wide area, it is best to replace the entire roof. But if the damage is only in patches, it is worth just replacing the slates.

Technique

Where you have to replace several slates together, you can refix the lower ones by nailing them into the battens as usual, working up the roof. It will, however, be impossible to nail in the final slates. These will be held in place with strips of lead, called tingles. These are also used to hold isolated slates in place, where these have slipped out.

Nail the tingle to the batten or board that is showing between the two slates below the one being fixed. The tingle should be of sufficient length so that when the slate is pushed back into position, the protruding end of the tingle can be bent up and over the bottom edge of the slate to hold it firmly in place.

When positioning the slate, make sure it is pushed up far enough so that its top edge rests on top of the next batten up. This will prevent the lower edge of the slate from lifting in a gale and working loose.

If a slate has broken, but the top section remains fixed, you will need to use a slate ripper to remove it. Push the blade of the ripper up under the slate you want to remove and move the head of the tool to one side to hook around the fixing nail. Tug the handle of the ripper or hammer it downwards, either to cut through the nail or pull it out of place.

Slate advice

There are many different sizes of slates, so make sure you buy the correct ones. It is a good idea to get secondhand ones, if they are in reasonable condition. If necessary, however, you can trim slates to size with an angle grinder. Fix them with copper nails.

To release a damaged slate, cut through the fixing nails using a slate ripper. Slide out the damaged slate.

To fix a new slate, nail a strip of lead, zinc or copper to one of the battens between the exposed slates. Slide the new slate into position and secure it in place by folding up the bottom end of the metal strip.

How to repair a flat roof

By their very nature, flat roofs tend to present more problems than pitched ones. Although they should have been built with a slight fall to enable water to run off, pools of water tend to form on the surface. The wide variation in temperature to which a flat roof is subjected will often separate the covering layers and crack them. Inevitably, leaks will occur.

You can reduce any expansion and contraction by topping the roof with a layer of white solar-reflective stone chippings. In time, however, these tend to be washed away.

Sparse chippings

Where chippings are sparse or missing altogether, coat the roof with bitumen chipping compound and scatter fresh chippings over the surface, pressing them into the bitumen with a light wooden roller. This should give the roof a few years' extra life.

Water leak

With a water leak, remember that the point at which you notice the stain inside the roof may be some distance from the problem area. Because it is common for the felt layers to separate, water trickling through the top layer may travel some distance under the felt before appearing on the ceiling below.

Inspection

When you inspect a flat roof, there are some general signs of potential problems to watch out for. If the top layer of felt has started to wrinkle or looks mottled, these are sure signs the covering is reaching the end of its useful life. Watch too for any signs of springiness in the roof decking; this indicates that chipboard decking has begun to break up. Also check the upstands where the roof meets an abutment, like the wall of an adjacent building or a parapet wall.

This initial inspection should give you a good picture of what needs to be done and how to proceed. You will probably have the option of carrying out a patch repair to the damaged area, applying an all-over treatment to the surface, or stripping off and replacing the roof.

Small repairs

If the problem demands only a patch repair over a hole, it is best to use metal-backed self-adhesive flashing strip, although a piece of roofing felt coated with cold bitumen would be a suitable alternative.

Scrape away any stones from the damaged area, then apply the liquid bitumen primer supplied with the flashing strip. When this has dried, peel the backing paper away from the flashing strip, which should be cut large enough to allow plenty of overlay, and press it into place, rolling it down with a wooden wallpaper seam roller.

BLISTERING

Your problem may just be blistering on the surface. In this case, make a star-shaped cut through the blister using a sharp trimming knife. Then peel back the edges of the blister to expose the underfelt. Coat the area with bitumen roofing compound and fold the flaps back in place, pressing them down with the roller.

CHECK FOR PROBLEMS

When you are up on the roof, check whether you can find any other existing or imminent problems. Obviously, if you notice a leak inside, you will not wait for a general inspection before carrying out necessary repairs.

To repair small splits and blisters in felted roofs, open up the top layer of the felt with two knife cuts at right angles. Peel back the tongues and spread some bituminous mastic over the repair (left). Then fix the tongues back down securely with galvanised clout nails and cover the repair with a felt patch, bedded on more mastic and rolled down with a wallpaper seam roller or similar tool.

How to waterproof a flat roof

Waterproofing a flat roof is a good way to protect the covering and guard against water penetration after specific repairs have been carried out. This is also good practice for added protection even if there are no obvious signs of damage to the roof. Better to be safe than sorry.

Layering

If you decide to apply an all-over surface treatment, there are various materials you can use. The principle is to apply an initial layer of liquid proofing to the roof surface, which you can reinforce with non-rotting fabric mesh, and then another layer, allowing it to solidify and form a tough, waterproof yet flexible sheet.

1

First remove any stone chippings and moss or algae from the surface. It is a good idea to apply a suitable fungicide to kill any remaining traces of growth.

2

Then apply the first coat of liquid proofing, using a soft broom.

3

If you are using reinforcing mesh, unroll it into the wet waterproofing and stipple it into the surface using a wet brush. Overlap the edges of adjacent strips by about 50mm (2in).

4

When the first coat has dried, apply a second one all over the roof and then a third. You can give this last coat extra protection with a covering of white reflective stone chippings or sharp sand, which you should apply while the final coating is still slightly tacky.

How to repair flashings

Flashings, which can be of lead or other corrosion-resistant metal or sometimes cement mortar, waterproof the join between the roof and adjacent brickwork, such as a chimney stack or the house wall. It is important that they remain in good condition. Repairs should be carried out when necessary.

For missing flashings, lay out some flashing tape, peel off the release paper and bed it in place.

Metal flashings are far superior to the mortar type, but after a time even they can corrode, tear or lift away from the wall, allowing water to trickle down behind them.

If flashing has simply lifted away from the roof, tap it back in place with a piece of wood. If it has pulled away at the top, where it is tucked into a mortar joint along the wall, the job of repairing it will involve more work.

Loose flashings

Where metal flashings have pulled away from a roof/wall junction, rake out the old mortar along the chase into which the flashing fitted. Then reposition the flashing, wedging it into the chase, and repoint with fresh mortar.

Missing flashings

If the flashing is porous or is missing altogether, fit a length of self-adhesive flashing tape. Brush on the special primer first and leave it to become tacky. Then cut the flashing tape to length, peel off the release paper and bed the tape in place along the junction. Tamp it down with a block of wood and a hammer to ensure that it forms a good bond.

How to repair chimneys

It is vitally important to keep chimneys in good order, especially in older properties. With the widespread use of central heating and rarity of log fires, many chimneys are now an uneccessary adjunct to a property. A loose part of a stack may be prone to collapse in high winds and other inclement weather, which may lead to untold damage to property (or people) below.

Never attempt any repairs to chimneys unless the stack is small and easy to reach from a roof ladder or you have hired proper chimney scaffolding.

Repointing

Because chimney stacks are in a very exposed position, it is common for the pointing between the bricks to crumble away. This can lead to dampness and make the stack unstable. Damaged joints will need to be repointed.

First rake out the old mortar to a depth of about 20mm (¾ in) and lightly wet the joints. A garden sprayer is ideal for this. Then press fresh mortar in place and smooth it off at a slight downward angle. The mortar should consist of one part cement to five parts sharp sand, with a little PVA adhesive added to improve its adhesion and workability.

Flaunching

Another vulnerable spot is the mortar (called flaunching) around the chimney pots. If there are cracks but the pots themselves are still held firmly in place, you can fill them by injecting non-setting mastic.

If, however, the flaunching is loose, you will have to chip it away – with care – and replace it with new mortar. Use one part cement to four parts sharp sand, again with a little PVA adhesive. Spread the mortar around the pots, building it up around the base and smoothing it so that it slopes down to the edges of the stack. This will allow any rainwater to drain off easily.

Pots

Cracked chimney pots can sometimes be repaired with silicone mastic; otherwise they will have to be replaced. If you have an old house, you may be able to get suitable pots from a demolition contractor or architectural salvage yard. To fit the new pot, chip away the old flaunching and replace it with new mortar, as described above.

If the flues are no longer used, you can fit ventilator caps to the pots to prevent rain getting in. Alternatively, you can remove the pots and make the flues rainproof by bedding airbricks around the sides at the top and laying paving slabs over the flues to throw rainwater clear of the stack. The airbricks ensure a gentle supply of air to the flues to keep them dry.

Repair minor cracks in the flaunching securing the pots to the stack using exterior-quality silicone mastic.

Flashings

Metal flashings and back gutters can also be a source of damp problems around chimney stacks (see page 117).

Chimney protection

Once repairs to the chimney stack have been completed, it is a good idea to paint the brickwork and the flaunching with silicone water-repellent sealer to prevent rain penetration and help protect against frost damage. The sealer dries colourless and does not affect the appearance of the stack.

Replace the flaunching with fresh mortar, mixed to a stiff consistency and laid about 50mm (2in) thick round the base of the pot.

How to fix guttering problems

It is important to keep guttering systems in good condition, since leaking or overflowing gutters will cause damp walls, stained interior decorations and possibly rotting of the fascias, soffit boards and rafter ends.

When checking or repairing the guttering, use a ladder fitted with a stay, which will hold the top clear of the gutter. If you are replacing any of the system, you should use a scaffold tower.

Checking guttering

The best time to check gutters and downpipes is when it is raining. Then you can see clearly if there are any leaking joints or whether the system is blocked anywhere and therefore overflowing. Make sure the inside of the guttering is free of debris. Clean the inside of metal gutters with a wire brush and paint the surface with black bituminous paint. Pour a bucket of water into the guttering and check that it drains freely and does not collect in pools.

Common problems

Gutters, especially old cast-iron ones, suffer from a range of common problems. The easiest to cure is the simple blockage, caused by debris washed off the roof surface or blown in by the wind, and resulting in water overflowing and running down the house walls.

Other problems include leaks from faulty joints, from cracks and splits caused by rust or accidental damage, and overflows due to sagging gutter brackets.

Replacing gutters

Where gutters are in very poor condition, it is often quicker to replace them completely with a new run of guttering, rather than to attempt a series of repairs.

If there are drainage problems, these can only be corrected by realigning the gutters. This is not an easy job and it is better to discard the existing system and fit new plastic guttering, or reproduction cast-iron gutters if you are restoring a period house.

gutter blocked by debris

Gutters blocked by debris can cause water to back up and overflow.

gutter damaged by ladder

Be careful when leaning ladders on guttering as this can cause damage.

gutter sagging at bracket

Watch for brackets that become loose, causing guttering to sag.

gutter outlet blocked

If the junction of guttering and downpipe becomes blocked by leaves, water cannot escape into the sewerage system below ground.

How to unblock drains and pipes

Leaves and other debris will sometimes accumulate in exterior drains and pipes. Unchecked, this can quickly lead to problems with overflowing water. This is particularly unpleasant when the blockage affects waste pipes and will likely cause problems for your neighbours as well. This is how to remedy the problem.

The main soil pipe will run vertically either inside or outside the house. If it is blocked, your best chance of clearing it will be to unscrew an inspection hatch and then to use either an auger or drain rods to dislodge the blockage.

Using an auger

A large auger (boring instrument) is used to clear blocked underground drains. It is passed down through an open gully and along the drain until the blockage is reached.

! AUTUMN WATCH

Always check your downpipes, drains and gutters each autumn when falling leaves may cause blockages. That way you can clear the area before the collection of debris worsens.

Using drain rods

These are used for clearing drains when there is a blockage between one (full) inspection chamber and the next (empty) one. When you discover the empty chamber, go back to the last full one and rod from there. Drain rod sets come with a choice of heads – plungers to push the blockage along the pipe, scrapers to pull it back, and wormscrews or cleaning wheels to dislodge it.

Start with a wormscrew connected to two rods, lowering it to the bottom of the chamber. Feel for the half-round channel at the bottom of the chamber and push the wormscrew along this until it enters the drain at the end. Push it along the drain, adding more rods to the free end, and only turn the rods clockwise, otherwise they may become unscrewed. Keep working at the obstruction until water flows into the empty chamber, then use the scraper and plunger to clear the underground drain section.

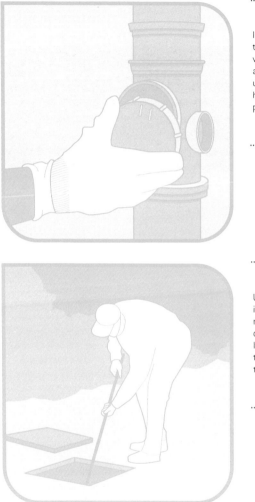

If you suspect that the blockage is in the vertical soil pipe, or at its base, begin by unscrewing an inspection hatch. Wear gloves and protective clothing.

Use drain rods in an inspection chamber to remove a blockage. You can hire a set from a local tool-hire company; they will come with all the necessary fittings.

TIP 61

How to fix a leaking gutter joint

If joints in plastic guttering are leaking, the only satisfactory solution is to dismantle them and fit new neoprene gaskets. If you have metal or asbestos cement guttering, the best method is to saw – from the underside – through the bolt and nut holding the sections together to ease the joint apart. Then clean it out, pack it with non-setting mastic and refix it with a new galvanised gutter bolt and nut.

Small repairs

There is an easier repair that may sometimes work. First scrape out the joint on each side. When it is thoroughly dry, inject a bead of non-setting exterior mastic into the crack. Finally, make sure of the repair by sticking a patch of self-adhesive flashing strip inside the gutter to form a complete seal.

CRACKS AND SPLITS

Any gutters or downpipes that are cracked or split should be replaced with new sections. However, you can make a temporary repair by covering the affected area with a patch of self-adhesive flashing strip applied over a coating of primer. Metal and asbestos-cement gutters and downpipes can also be repaired with glass fibre paste, as used for car body repairs.

CORROSION

You can also use self-adhesive flashing strip to effect a temporary repair to badly corroded cast-iron and steel gutters and downpipes. However, these can be dangerous if they fall off the wall, so it is better to replace them with new cast-iron or steel guttering or with the lightweight plastic type.

Fitting guttering and downpipes

Plastic gutters are fixed by being clipped into brackets screwed to the fascia board. In theory, they will drain if fixed level. In practice, however, it is best to fit them with a slight fall of about 25mm (1in) in 15m (50ft).

When fitting a downpipe, always work from the outlet. Start by fitting an offset to bring the downpipe back to the face of the wall. Working downwards from the offset bracket, fit the downpipe into the required number of bracket clips to hold it firmly against the wall.

If you are replacing damaged plastic gutter or downpipe sections, note that the various systems are not interchangeable, so it is best to stick to what you have.

Above left: To repair a leaking but otherwise sound joint, scrape out any old sealing compound and re-seal the joint with mastic.

Left: If this fails to work, undo the joint by hacksawing through the nut underneath. Then separate the joint sections, reassemble them on a generous bed of mastic and remake the joint with a new nut and bolt. As a stopgap measure, try sealing the joint by bedding a piece of self-adhesive flashing tape over it. If a plastic gutter joint leaks, dismantle the joint by removing the clips and fit a new sealing gasket.

How to repair and protect brickwork

The most common fault in brickwork is deterioration in the mortar joints, when the mortar often flakes, cracks and crumbles. Old age and excessive weathering are common causes, especially if the initial mortar mix used was too weak for the job. Cracks in the mortar joints allow rainwater to penetrate. In winter this can freeze, causing the crack to widen and the mortar to decay.

Repointing

To repoint damaged joints, first rake out the old mortar and then insert a new mix. This is normally made up of one part cement, one part hydrated powder lime and six parts soft sand. The lime makes the mix more workable, but you can substitute it with a few drops of a proprietary liquid plasticiser. If you make the mix stronger by increasing the proportion of cement, the mortar is liable to shrink and crack as it dries. It will also impede the drying of the wall when wet.

If you are only repointing a few joints, then you can buy bags of mortar mix to which you simply add water. Tip out the entire content and mix it thoroughly together, then put back into the bag what you do not need. The ingredients tend to separate and if you only tip out what you need you may well get too much or too little cement.

Weatherproofing

If some bricks are spalling, the rest are probably porous and will need protection. The easiest method is to apply a silicone water-repellent sealer with a brush, spray or roller.

Apply a water-repellent sealer to protect your brickwork.

How to replace brickwork

Old age and frost damage can cause brickwork to become porous, eventually allowing damp to pass through to the inside of the house. One solution is to patch up broken or spalled bricks with mortar, colour-matched to the surrounding ones. This is, however, difficult to do well. And if you have any cracks or gaps between the patching mortar and the brick, water can be sucked in by capillary action, causing further spalling problems.

A better solution is to chop out the offending brick and replace it. This might sound complicated but it can be achieved in four fairly easy steps.

1

Where frost has damaged the surface of a brick, drill a series of holes into it to a depth of about 100mm (4in) with a power drill and masonry bit.

2

Chop out the honeycombed brick and surrounding mortar with a cold chisel and club hammer, and clean up the recess.

3

Apply ready-mixed bricklaying mortar, worked to a stiff consistency, to the top of the brick below and on the sides and frog (the V-shaped indentation) of the new brick. Push it firmly into place.

Use a chisel to chop out the brick and surrounding mortar.

4

Tamp it in flush with its neighbours, press more mortar in round it and neaten off the joints to match the wall's style of pointing.

How to fill and patch rendering

Rendering is the layer of plaster that covers the brickwork on your house. It is essential to have rendering to protect the brickwork from penetrating damp. Over time, cracks will appear or rendering will 'blow'. These faults must be repaired. This is how to do so.

Filling rendering

You often find hairline crazing in a rendered wall. Such a superficial situation is easily overcome with a coat of good exterior wall paint. Small cracks must be filled, but any repair will be obvious until the wall is painted.

1

When treating cracks, you must first chip away all loose material and under-cut the cracks to ensure the filler is well anchored and will not fall out later. Then dust out the cavity and dampen it with water.

2

To fill the crack, you can use either an exterior grade filler or mortar mix. The former is convenient but only economical for small areas. Dry mortar mix can be obtained in small quantities or you can make your own using one part cement, one part hydrated powder lime and six parts sand. You can of course use a proprietary liquid plasticiser in place of the lime.

Top Tip

Cracks often occur in rendering at natural breaks – in line with the corners of door and window frames, for example.

Patching rendering

If rendering is coming away from the wall, the cause may be dampness, a fault in the rendering mix or defective brickwork joints. This is often evidenced by bulges, where it has 'blown' or, in other words, lost contact with the wall.

Tap suspect areas lightly with a hammer. If there is a fault, the rendering will fall away and you must clean off the affected area with a bolster chisel and club hammer until you reach rendering that adheres firmly to the wall.

A rendering mix consists of one part cement, one part lime and six parts sand. The lime makes the rendering more flexible and easier to use. But it must be applied quickly, since after mixing you have only 15 or 20 minutes until it becomes too firm to work. Do not add water to a setting mix since this will only weaken it.

TECHNIQUE

For normal house work you should appy two coats of rendering. The first should be thick and the second, top coat a skim of 6mm (¼ in) thickness.

1

If you try to dab the mix on the wall it will just fall off again. The idea is to apply it with a sweeping motion. Always work from the bottom of the patch upwards with the first coat. When this is starting to set, scratch it to form a key for the second coat to grip.

2

Allow 24 hours before applying the second coat, starting from the top this time and working from left to right with the same flowing movement.

3

When complete, level off with the surrounding wall surface. Leave this until it is almost dry before drawing a trowel, dampened with water, across it to give a smooth, flat finish.

To repair cracks in rendering, first chip away all loose material along the line of the crack, under-cutting it to provide a better key for the repair mortar.

Force mortar into the crack and trowel it off level with the wall surface.

How to paint exterior walls

Paint helps protect your home from wind, rain and sun. That is why the outside needs redecorating about every four years, or more often if you live near the sea or in an industrial area. It's best to paint at the end of the summer, when wood has had a long period in which to dry out.

PAINTING ADVICE

Choose bright, still days if you can, following the sun on the house so that the paint is dried, but avoid painting in full sunlight or when it's windy. It's dangerous to use a ladder in high winds, and paint splashes on walls, caused by wind, can be very difficult to remove.

Preparation for painting

→ Tie back climbing plants.

→ Check the state of roof and guttering and repair any leaks.

→ Check for rot on fascias and barge-boards beneath the eaves, windows, doors (especially the base) and decorative wood. Replace where necessary, or repair by scraping back to sound wood, removing flaking paint and filling any cracks with exterior stopper.

→ If rendering is falling apart, cut it back until you reach the part that is sound, then clean it and patch with mortar. Large areas will need professional attention.

→ Clean out defective pointing and fill large cracks with ready-mixed mortar, small ones with exterior filler.

→ To remove dirt on painted walls, brush with a stiff brush from the top down. Treat mould with one part bleach to four of water. Leave for two days and then brush the mould away with a stiff brush. Apply stabilising solution to flaky patches.

→ Replace any cracked window panes and leave for two weeks before painting the frame, because the putty needs time to harden. Fill gaps between the wall and window frame with flexible exterior filler.

→ Scrape metal downpipes and gutters and clean with a wire brush to remove flaking paint. Apply anti-rust primer to any rusty patches that remain. Sand sound paintwork lightly to provide a key.

→ Remove peeling paint from window frames and fill and prime where necessary.

→ Strip peeling varnish to the bare wood, sand, and apply a sealer coat of varnish thinned with white spirit.

→ Clean, sand and dust off sound paintwork.

Order of painting

1

Paint fascias, barge-boards and gutters.

2

Paint walls in sections, starting in a corner and working from top to bottom.

3

Paint downpipes.

4

Paint windows and doors.

Painting wood and metalwork

Use gloss paint or stains on wood and gloss on metal. It's important to make sure they are suitable for outdoor use. In most cases, this means using a solvent-based paint, which is more weather resistant. But although paint systems especially designed for exterior use may specify two coats of undercoat plus one of liquid gloss for maximum durability, it's often possible to use non-drip one-coat products too – check the recommendations on the tin. Start from the top and work down, placing a piece of board behind downpipes to protect the wall from the paint.

Painting walls

Before you start, wrap downpipes in polythene or newspaper to protect them from paint splatters and cover plants and paths with plastic sheeting. Start by 'cutting in' – painting a narrow strip – next to barge-boards, doors and windows. Change to a wide wall brush for small areas, a long-pile roller for large ones, and apply the masonry paint with a criss-cross movement. Work from the top down in bands about an arm's length in width, and overlap each strip when you move on, for even coverage. Make sure you don't lean out too far when working at height.

How to cast concrete

Ready-mixed concrete is one of the most versatile building materials available to the do-it-yourselfer. It is an essential ingredient of many building projects, in the form of strip or raft foundations set in the ground to support walls and other structures. It is also a constructional material in its own right, and can be used to create many outdoor features such as patios, paths and drives.

In principle, laying concrete in the form of a patio, path or drive is little different from casting a slab foundation. However, there are several specific points to bear in mind over and above the straightforward casting technique.

Get organised

Firstly, order all the ready-mixed concrete you need for the job in one delivery. If you use several batches of concrete for a large project, slight differences in shade will be impossible to correct.

Layout

You may want to create shapes rather more elaborate than straightforward rectangles and squares. Fortunately, concrete can do this easily so long as you are prepared to spend some time setting out the formwork in the shape you require.

Obstacles

As you plan the layout of your project, watch out for obstacles such as manhole covers and drainage gullies. You will need to plan the levels of your new surfaces carefully unless you are willing to move or reposition the obstacle.

Division of area

Large areas of concrete cannot be laid as continuous slabs, or they will crack due to expansion and contraction. This means dividing the work up into bays, each separated from its neighbour by an expansion joint of hardboard or bituminous felt if the concrete is laid as a continuous operation. If it is laid in alternate bays, board or felt joints are not needed; a simple butt joint will suffice.

Work the concrete into the sides and corners to avoid hollows.

Use a steel float to apply the finishing texture.

1

When the concrete arrives, try to have it delivered direct to where it is needed via the chute on the lorry.

2

Use a wheelbarrow to transport loads to areas the chute cannot reach. Protect glazed doors with a sheet of hardboard.

3

Spread the concrete using a garden rake and a shovel. Work it well into the sides and corners of the formwork to avoid hollows.

4

Cast the slab in easily managed bays no more than 3m (10ft) long and compact the mix down well with a tamping beam.

5

Lay the next bay in the same way, finishing off with a sawing to-and-fro action of the beam to level the surface of the slab.

6

When you have compacted the slab, apply the finishing texture. For a smooth, polished surface use a steel float.

How to repair concrete paving

Paths and patios do not last forever. The concrete paving slabs can become cracked or the mortar that holds them in place erodes away. Follow these steps to maintain your concrete path or patio.

Concrete paving slabs are a common choice of surfacing for patios. The same slabs can also be used for paths, but for drives, stronger and thicker, hydraulically pressed slabs must be laid on a much stronger base. Normally, paving slabs are set on dabs of mortar on a sand base, but they may also be laid on a solid bed of mortar, a method that is always used when laying heavy-duty slabs for a drive.

A slab may have broken because something too heavy has been placed on it or as a result of something hitting it. Sometimes, individual slabs may become loose or may sink, in which case they will need to be lifted and re-laid.

1

If the joints around the slab have been filled with mortar, the first job will be to chip this out.

2

If possible, remove a broken slab from the centre, working outwards; you can use a bolster chisel or a garden spade to lever up sections or whole slabs.

3

Clean out the bottom of the hole and level it using builder's sand tamped down with a stout piece of wood — allow about 10mm (½ in) for the mortar. Mix up a batch of mortar and put down five dabs, one in the centre and one near each corner. Also lay a fillet of mortar along each edge.

4

Lower the new slab, or the old slab if it is undamaged, into position.

5

Tap it down with the handle of a club (spalling) hammer. Check that the slab is level with its neighbours by placing a spirit level across them.

6

Fill the joints with more mortar.

Lift out the broken pieces, or lever them up with a bolster chisel or spade, but protect the edges of adjoining slabs with pieces of wood.

Add some more mortar to finish the joints, smoothing it down level with the paving. Brush off the excess immediately, otherwise it will stain the surface of the paving.

How to lay decking

Some extravagant wooden decks feature balustrade surrounds and stairs leading into the garden, but if you simply wish to build a simple square deck, follow the 14-stage process listed here.

1

Using a tape measure, mark off equal distances for the lag bolt holes. Check to make sure the joist and deck board will be below the doorstep to prevent rainwater from running in.

2

When choosing the positions of the bolt holes, avoid the mortar joints – the brickwork will provide a far better fixing. Wood drill through the wood, then use a masonry drill to penetrate the brick.

3

Hammer a rawl bolt through the timber and into the wall. Make sure the nut is on before you hammer it home, otherwise it will burr over and the nut will not fit.

4

Tighten the nut with an adjustable spanner until the nut starts to be drawn in the timber and the wood is tight to the wall. Check the level.

5

Fix the first joist to the ledger board, making sure that the top edges of each timber are level with each other.

6

The outer joists can be attached with screws, which should be long enough to go through the first timber and into the other by at least 25mm (1in).

7

With a builder's square or large set square. line up the last joint and fix with a screw; then check that all the other corners are at 90 degrees. If the deck is square, the diagonal measurements will be equal.

8

Measure out and fix supporting joists at 400mm (16in) centres. Fix from each side by screwing in at an angle. If no edging is required, this method can be used to hide the screws from view.

9

Measure and cut two rows of noggins to stretch across the beams. Alternate their

position so that you can get the nails in. Use screws on the outside of the deck frame and nails on the area hidden by the deck boards. Place the noggins on the ground to provide extra support to the frame (above).

10

Screw the first deck board into position. Make sure it is parallel to the first joist as this will set the pattern for the rest of the boards.

11

Use a 5mm spacer such as a spanner to set an even distance between each deck board. This will allow room for the timber to expand when it is wet.

12

Once the ends of the deck boards have been fixed down, the rest of the deck can be screwed down. Use a chalk line to line all the screws up together.

13

If the deck boards are warped, insert the 5mm spacer between the boards and use a chisel to lever the boards to the correct position. Then screw in the boards (left).

14

To finish the edge, screw down a length of board to use as a straight edge. Make sure the distance between the board and the circular saw blade is such that the saw will cut the decking boards flush to the joist. Run the saw along to trim the ends of the deck board to a uniform length.

How to repair a fence

All timber fences will require some sort of maintenance or repair during their lifetime. This might consist of dealing with rotten timber or stabilising the fence. Whatever the problem, it should be dealt with promptly.

Spurring a post

On most timber fences it is the posts that determine stability and the chances are that the bulk of repairs will have to be made to these. As fence posts are bedded in the ground, a relatively common occurrence is rotting. However, this doesn't necessarily require that the whole post is replaced. You can secure the sound timber to a concrete fence spur that serves as an anchor and is fixed in the ground in the same way as a post. Check that the spur is upright, and that its longer face is against the post. Use the pre-drilled holes in the spur as a template and transfer them on to the post. You'll then have to drill holes in the posts and bind the two together using coach bolts.

METAL SPIKE

Perhaps the simplest method of stabilising a rotted post is to refix it using a special metal spike. All you do is drive the spike into the ground and then fix the post into its socket, after trimming away the rotten section.

Gravel boards

If you have a gravel board that has rotted, then replace it without delay to avoid the danger of the vertical boards being attacked by the damp.

First you should remove the rotten boards, then clear away the soil that will hinder you from fixing the new ones in position. Some gravel boards are fixed into recesses cut in the fence posts; others are nailed to blocks called 'cleats' fixed to the bottom of the posts. If necessary, cut new cleats from 50mm sq (2in sq) timber. These should be 150mm (6in) long and you'll have to nail them to the inside faces of the posts. Use 150 x 25mm (6 x 1in) timber for the new gravel board. Nail to the blocks and check that there is no soil piling against the board.

Concrete post

Your fence might have concrete posts, in which case you'll have to cut longer fixing blocks, about 600mm (24in) in length. Drive these into the soil so that they butt up tightly against the inside face of the post. Make sure that only 150mm (6in) of the pegs project from the ground, then nail the board in position.

Replacing boards

It is possible that on a close-boarded fence individual boards will have to be replaced. Start by removing the old one and extracting the old nails. If this is impossible, drive them into the arris rail. Then punch through the nails holding the thicker, outer edge of the adjacent board before slipping the thinner edge of the new board under it. You can then nail through the two boards and through the thick edge of the new board where it overlaps the previous one.

Panel fences

With panel fences, repairs are not quite so simple, especially with interwoven fencing. It is not easy to obtain individual slats to fit into a panel and to do so you'll probably have to remove a slat from a damaged panel. If you don't have any damaged panels, ask at a local garden centre.

To replace a slat, lay the damaged panel on firm dry ground. Remove the central vertical support band on the upper side and one of the two battens at each end. Carefully remove the damaged slat and replace it with the new one, taking care not to disturb the position of the other slats. You can then replace the vertical battens and fix the panel back into position. A simpler method would be to replace the entire panel: proceed as if you were erecting a new panel fence.

A damaged board in a panel of horizontal closeboarded fencing can be replaced.

After marking through the holes in the spur and drilling through the post, bolt them together with coach bolts before concreting in.

Removing a rotten fence board by punching the fixing nails through into the arris rail; support the rail from behind.

Plumbing and Heating

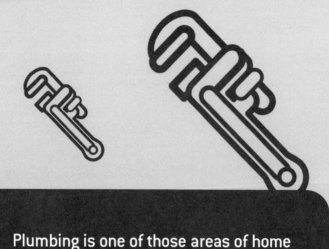

Plumbing is one of those areas of home maintenance that is sometimes best left to an expert tradesman. If you are not confident about the workings of your water system, meddling could lead to further problems. However, there are a number of relatively simple jobs that any homeowner should master. If you are able to fix a leaking tap, mend the flush on your toilet cistern and fit a thermostat for a radiator you will save considerable money on plumber's fees.

How to fit a washing machine

Companies that supply washing machines to the householder will usually fit the appliance for an additional fee, but if you are competent with basic plumbing there is no reason why you should not tackle this job yourself.

Plumbing in a washing machine is quite a simple operation. The water supply comes from the rising main for cold water and from the nearest hot water supply pipe.

The easiest way to break into an existing pipe is to use a self-cutting valve. You should fit this in a suitable position around the appropriate pipe, which you should first clean with wet and dry abrasive paper. You then tighten the screws holding the two halves of the valve together so that the clamp firmly grips the pipe. By screwing the body of the valve tightly and quickly home, you will cut through the pipe and thus release water to flow through the valve.

By using this method, you not only make it easy to break into the supply system but also create an emergency shut-off valve should you ever need to stop the water supply to the washing machine. You then run your pipework from these valves to a convenient position at the rear of the washing machine.

Cold water supply

When installing the cold water supply from the rising main, you must fit a double-check valve before the shut-off valve to prevent back-siphonage, unless the machine itself incorporates one. You then screw the hoses from the washing machine tightly by hand on to the threaded ends of the valves.

Connecting up

The drain hose from the machine can be hooked into a vertical piece of drainpipe with a trap fitted at the bottom. This pipe should be a minimum 600mm (24in) in length. Finally, connect an outlet pipe from the trap through the exterior wall either directly into the drainage stack or to discharge into a convenient gully.

It is important to leave an air gap around the top of the vertical pipe and the hose from the machine. If there is no gap, the water could be siphoned out.

You can also connect hoses direct to special traps fitted beneath the kitchen sink waste outlet.

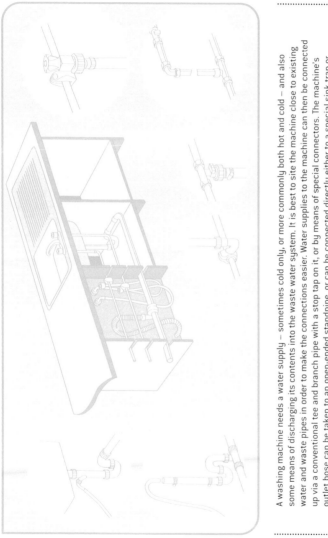

A washing machine needs a water supply – sometimes cold only, or more commonly both hot and cold – and also some means of discharging its contents into the waste water system. It is best to site the machine close to existing water and waste pipes in order to make the connections easier. Water supplies to the machine can then be connected up via a conventional tee and branch pipe with a stop tap on it, or by means of special connectors. The machine's outlet hose can be taken to an open-ended standpipe, or can be connected directly either to a special sink trap or to the sink waste pipe using a special connector.

How to mend a dripping tap

Dripping taps leave stains on baths and basins, and waste water. If the tap is dripping from the spout, the leak is probably caused by a worn washer, which is relatively easy to replace.

1

Turn off the water supply to the tap, either at the stop valve on the pipe running to it, the gate valve in the loft or airing cupboard, or at the main stoptap. If you turn the water off at the stoptap, you'll need to drain the system before you start to work, to stop water pouring out. That means turning all the taps on until they run dry and you may also have to switch off the immersion heater, or central-heating boiler (if you have a 'wet' central-heating system).

! SUPATAP

It isn't necessary to drain the system if the tap you're working on is a Supatap (reverse pressure tap), which turns off the water internally when the tap casing is removed.

2

If the tap has a standard (capstan) head, loosen the little screw in the side, if there is one, and unscrew the top part of the casing beneath by twisting it anti-clockwise to reveal the tap head. If the casing is very stiff, wrap the tap with a thick cloth to protect the chrome plating and use an adjustable wrench for extra power (opposite, top right).

If the tap has a shrouded head, the head and casing form a single piece. There's no one way of removing it, so first look to see if there's a screw in the head (this is sometimes hidden by a flap that can be prised off). If there's no obvious way of removing the head, pull it to see if the head comes away. If it doesn't, turn the tap on full and carry on twisting to see if that works.

3

Holding the tap firmly, unscrew the large nut inside with a spanner, turning it anti-clockwise (you may need to oil the nut first). This frees the 'headgear' that contains the washer.

4

Detach the 'jumper' rod, which has a disc or nut at the base holding the washer in place. Prise off the disc to remove the washer, or oil the nut if necessary, and unscrew it with a spanner. Remove the old washer and examine it. If it's a conventional flat washer, you can use a standard replacement. If it has a special domed or curved shape, you may need to contact a specialist supplier. If you can't undo this nut, you can buy a new jumper complete with washer.

5

Fit the new tap washer. Standard sizes for sink and basin taps are 15mm (½ in) and 20mm (¾ in), and 25mm (1in) for bath taps.

6

Put the tap back together and turn on the water supply.

How to fix a cistern valve

If you discover water running from the outside overflow pipe of your toilet cistern, the trouble will lie with the cistern valve, which will need replacing. This should be dealt with as soon as possible, especially during winter since the outside pipe could freeze up and this might lead to indoor flooding.

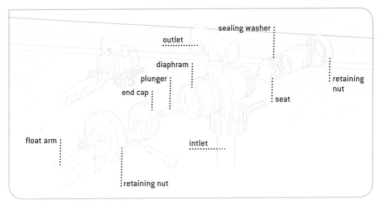

Modern valves generally have plastic bodies, and contain a diaphragm that is pressed against the inlet valve by the float arm, instead of a piston and washer. If they give trouble, it is usually the diaphragm that needs replacing. To do this, dismantle the valve after turning off the water supply.

1

First take off the top of the cistern and look at the valve. It will be either a piston-operated type (the Portsmouth valve) or a diaphragm type (the Garston valve). In either case, the first thing to do is turn off the water supply.

The more up-to-date Garston valve is fitted either through the side of the cistern or, with more modern versions, at the top of the plastic tower that rises from the bottom of the cistern. The water is discharged from above the valve to prevent any possibility of back siphonage. Although there are some slight variations of this valve now on the market, the same basic instructions apply as far as maintenance and repair work is concerned.

2

To gain access to the valve, you must undo the large serrated plastic nut nearest the float. This nut sometimes locks on to the body. If so, pour boiling water over it to try and release it. If this does not work, you may have to use a self-grip wrench on the nut and another wrench on the body. Turn it anti-clockwise, looking from the float end.

3

You can now remove the diaphragm to inspect it and, if punctured or damaged in any way, replace it. Check the plastic seat it presses against, which should be smooth, clear and without any scratches or grooves. If the seat is faulty, you can remove it by unscrewing the other large nut on the body. Make sure the new seat you fit has a hole the same size. Before

reassembling the valve, lubricate the threads with petroleum jelly. Use only hand pressure (no wrenches) when replacing the nuts so that you do not damage the threads.

4

To adjust the water level, never try to bend the float arm. If you have a tower valve, first check that the support screw at the opposite side to the float arm is resting lightly but firmly against the side of the cistern. This is to stop the tower bending with the pressure from the float. If it is not touching the side, loosen the locknut and turn the screw by hand until it is in firm contact with the side of the cistern. Then tighten up the locknut.

5

You will see that the float arm is fixed to a pivot bracket with a locknut on either side. To alter the level, slacken one locknut and tighten the other, thus moving the float arm through the bracket. To lower the level, move the arm towards the valve and in the opposite direction to raise it.

QUICK CURE

One frequent piece of advice is to bend down the rod or arm connected to the float. This may provide a temporary cure, but it does not remedy the basic trouble in the valve.

How to fix a toilet flush

If the flush on your toilet is not working properly – either does not release water at all or requires several pumps on the handle to do so – there will almost certainly be a fault with the diaphragm. Here's how to replace one and return your toilet to full working order.

1

First check that the water level is correct. If not, adjust it as already described and try again. If it still does not work properly, turn off the water supply and flush the cistern fully. Then empty out all the remaining water with a jug, mopping up any left in the bottom with an old towel or cloth.

2

You must now disconnect the water supply and warning pipes and then undo and remove the wing nuts below the cistern. Check that the cistern is not screwed on to the wall and then lift it off. Do not lose the rubber gasket.

3

Disconnect the operating linkage from the handle and undo and remove the large backnut beneath the cistern that holds the siphon assembly in place. Lift out the siphon and you will see the old diaphragm on the plunger in the siphon tube. This will either be split or torn, so remove it.

4

Fit the new diaphragm, carefully trimming it to size as necessary with a sharp pair of scissors. It should fit well to the sides of the tube without dragging. Use the plunger as a guide. Then refit the plunger to the siphon, clean out any debris and use a non-setting mastic to assemble the siphon to the cistern. Screw the backnut up tight.

5

When assembling the cistern to the wc, do not forget the rubber gasket. Reconnect the water and warning pipes and the flush linkage and, finally, turn the water back on. Make sure that none of the joints leak. The cistern should now flush correctly.

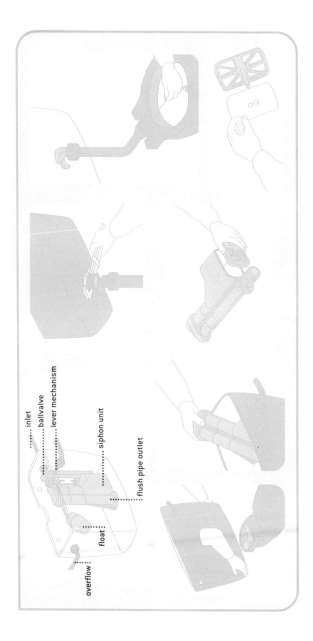

inlet

ballvalve

lever mechanism

siphon unit

flush pipe outlet

float

overflow

COMMON BATH PROBLEMS

You might not feel competent enough to fit a new bath, but there are other faults with fitted baths that, with a little know-how, you can rectify fairly easily. Bath staining and blocked bath traps are two common problems associated with baths. By following this advice, you will prevent these issues becoming a problem in your bathroom.

Staining

One problem sometimes inherited when moving into a house is staining below the bath taps where they have been allowed to drip continuously.

BATH CLEANER

In the case of a cast-iron or steel bath, the stain may respond to one of the more aggressive bath cleaners. Check these are suitable for use on enamel.

BATH PAINT

Another way of dealing with such stains is with special bath paint. If properly applied, this can be quite effective, but you must follow the manufacturers' instructions carefully to get good results.

Blocked bath trap

Another problem is a blocked bath trap, where the usual culprit is hair. To gain access to the trap normally means removing the panel at the side of the bath.

WOOD PANEL

Where this is of wood or hardboard, it is usually held in place by screws, sometimes mirror screws with chrome-plated dome-shaped heads that unscrew out of the main screw.

PLASTIC PANEL

Plastic panels tend to be clipped in place neatly underneath the rim of the bath.

COMMON SHOWER PROBLEMS

One of the most common problems with showers is when the head becomes blocked due to excess scale, particularly in hard water areas. Since this is a gradual process, it is not always noticed until the shower becomes really weak. Regular treatment here will eliminate any serious effects.

Blocked shower head

Take the head off the hose and, if possible, dismantle it. There are a number of descaling solutions available, which take varying amounts of time to work and are applied in different ways. Among these are some 'environmentally friendly' products that are less aggressive, but equally effective – and safer to use.

Alternatively, soak in a solution of white vinegar and water. Use an old toothbrush to dislodge stubborn limescale.

Descaling

While tackling this problem, you may be able to descale some of the working parts of the shower itself. But be careful if you have to put any parts of a thermostatically controlled shower into boiling water. Check first with the manufacturers' instructions.

Fitting a shower

If you are considering installing a shower, there are four basic types from which you can choose:

Mixer tap shower
This invoves replacing the bath taps with a mixer tap with a shower connection.

Thermostatic shower
This gives a better flow and control of water temperature.

Pumped shower
These are not dependent on a good head of water. The rose is adjustable to give variations in the pattern or volume of water spray.

Electric shower
The water is heated electrically as it passes through the shower. Because it takes a high current, it should be installed professionally.

How to fix water pressure/temperature problems

Because your water system feeds several different appliance in your house – from the washing machine and dishwasher, to taps and toilet flush – you may suffer from sudden changes in water pressure and temperature. This problem is particularly common with showers.

Weak output

If the shower is run from your domestic hot water system and the output is weak, it may be that there is insufficient head of water. Normally the minimum is 1m (3ft) vertical distance from the shower head at its highest position to the bottom of the cold water storage tank in the loft. There are two ways of improving the flow rate and getting a more powerful shower.

SOLUTION

The first is to install a pumped shower, the second is to raise the tank in your loft. This will involve disconnecting and extending the rising main, which takes water to the tank, and the supply outlets (normally two) from the tank. The tank itself will have to be moved on to a raised platform strong enough to support it. The height of this will depend on how much extra 'head' you need for your shower.

Temperature problems

One other problem frequently encountered with this type of shower is when someone turns on another tap in the house and the shower temperature changes dramatically. This is especially likely to happen with a bath mixer tap shower or one installed from the supply pipes feeding the bath.

RE-PLUMB

The only way to overcome this is to re-plumb the shower so that it takes its cold water direct from the storage tank, or if your water is heated by a combination boiler.

If you are going to carry out re-plumbing work, use 22mm ¾ in) diameter pipe and fit large bends to give the best possible flow. This solution may not completely eliminate the problem, but it will certainly greatly improve it.

How to fix a leaking or burst pipe

Where possible, water pipes should be insulated. In cold conditions, pipes are susceptible to freezing and cracking. Then, when the pipes thaw out, water leaks occur. If you do suffer a burst pipe, however, do not despair. It is relatively straightforward.

A burst pipe requires quick and effective action to both minimise the damage done by escaping water and to get the system back in use as soon as possible.

1

Turn off the water supply to the affected pipe immediately and pack thick cloths round the damage to staunch the flow while you drain it down. If the pipe is damaged because you have driven a nail through it, leave the nail in place until the pipe is drained.

2

Once the pipe is drained, cut out the affected section and fit a new piece. You can buy a repair kit comprising a length of flexible copper pipe with two push-fit polybutylene connectors to allow a quick replacement to be made.

Stopping a leak with a repair clamp; clip the two halves of the clamp together round the pipe and tighten the wing-nut.

TIP 78

How to deal with plumbing emergencies

Where plumbing is concerned, it pays to know a few emergency procedures. A household where the water supply does not work at all – no washing machine, hot bath, or central heating – is a point of crisis, especially during the cold winter months. But worse is a situation where the water cannot be turned off, which will quickly lead to severe flooding. Read the advice below and learn how to cope with four common plumbing emergencies.

Water pours from the loft

1

Turn the main stoptap off (clockwise). It is usually close to the kitchen sink (if you can't turn it off, see opposite). Put buckets under the leaks, then turn on all the cold taps in the house and flush all the WCs to drain the cold water storage cistern.

2

Find the cause of the trouble. It may be a burst pipe in the loft or a cistern overflow caused by a blocked overflow pipe.

Turn off the main stoptap.

No water comes from a tap

1

If no water flows from the kitchen sink cold tap, check that the main stoptap is open. If it is, call your water supply company. You will find the number under 'Water' in the phone book.

2

If no water flows from other taps, check the cold water cistern. It may have emptied because of a jammed ballvalve. If it is empty, move the float arm sharply up and down to free the valve. Alternatively, in frosty weather there may be an ice plug blocking a supply pipe. If the kitchen cold tap is working, check the flow into the cold water cistern by pressing down the ballvalve. If there is no inflow, the rising main is frozen, probably in the loft between the ceiling and cistern inlet.

3

If the cistern is filling, check the bathroom taps. If there is no flow from one tap, its supply pipe from the cistern is frozen.

4

To thaw a pipe, strip off any lagging from the affected part and apply hot water bottles. If a pipe is difficult to get at, blow warm air on to it with a hair dryer. **WARNING** Do not use a blowtorch to defrost a frozen pipe. It may cause a fire, or melt the solder in a pipe joint and cause another leak.

Hot water cylinder leaks

1

Turn off the gatevalve (clockwise) on the supply pipe from the cold water cistern to the hot water cylinder. If there is no gatevalve, turn off the main stoptap and turn on all the taps to empty the cistern.

2

Switch off the boiler and the electricity if you have exposed wires.

3

Connect a hose to the cylinder drain valve (near the base of the cylinder where the supply pipe from the cold water cistern enters). Put the other end of the hose into an outside drain.

4

Open up the drain valve with pliers (or a special drain valve key).

5

Get the hot water cylinder repaired or replaced by a plumber.

Cannot turn off the water

If you cannot turn off the water at the main stoptap, tie up the float arm in the cold water cistern to stop it filling, turn on all the taps (except the kitchen cold tap) and flush the WCs. Then call an emergency plumber.

There is also an outdoor stoptap – usually under a small metal plate in the pavement or driveway outside. If you cannot find or turn off the indoor stoptap, then use this tap. You will need a special stoptap key with a long handle.

How to fit a radiator thermostat

Thermostats are fitted instead of the ordinary radiator on/off valves. They control the flow of hot water to each radiator, and so can control the temperature of individual rooms – normally a hit-and-miss affair, since a room thermostat in, say, the living room, can hardly know whether a bedroom is too hot or too cold. They simplify alterations to the heating system, too, because you no longer have to rely on things like the size and number of radiators in a room to regulate its temperature.

1

Drain down the system and remove the old on/off valve plus radiator tail pipe and coupling nut.

2

Fit the tail pipe supplied with the new valve, binding its thread with PTFE sealing tape to ensure a watertight join, then connect the thermostatic radiator valve to this tail pipe, tightening up the coupling nut.

3

Finally, connect the radiator supply pipe to the new valve, shortening it if necessary, and fitting it with a new olive.

4

Recommission the system. Set the new valve for the required room temperature.

Fitting a thermostat head to a radiator is a relatively easy exercise that can save you money on your heating bills.

How to bleed a radiator

If radiators are hot at the bottom and cold at the top, they need bleeding. Keep an eye on the inlet valves, too. A slow leak is easily fixed, but can damage nearby flooring if left to drip.

Use a radiator drain key – obtainable from any hardware store – or a flat tip screwdriver to release air from the system.

In either case, turn anti-clockwise – no more than a quarter turn – and hold a cloth directly under the valve to catch any dirty water (see below). Air should vent from the valve, making a hissing noise. When water starts to come out, close the valve and wipe the area dry.

You can buy a small gadget for bleeding radiators that has an integral container for catching any drips.

Leaking

Leaks can occur between the valve tail (the short pipe to which the valve is connected) and the threaded inlet to the radiator itself. This can often be cured with a smear of silicone leak sealant. Run the radiator hot to dry out the leak, then apply the sealant. The leaking water will start it setting immediately, but you should leave the heat on for at least two hours to get a total seal.

How to fit a radiator

If you're looking into the central heating of your home, consider your radiators. Specifically, have you got enough and are they in the right place? If the answer to either question is no, given basic plumbing skills, you should be able to tackle the necessary alterations yourself.

Before doing repairs and alterations, you must drain the system of water, and it is worth knowing how to do this in any event, in case the system springs a leak. First turn off everything (including the boiler) to stop new water entering the system. Then drain the heating pipework. Fix a hosepipe to the draincock and direct the flow of water into, for instance, an outside drain.

New pipes

If the existing system is run in standard copper pipe, installing new radiators should be fairly easy. Begin by tracing the feed and return circuit pipes supplying existing radiators, and decide where to tap into them. If you are adding only one radiator, any convenient point will do. Break into each pipe with a compression or capilliary tee fitting, and run branch pipes to the new radiator connection.

Connections

Radiators come with a hole at each corner. The bottom two take an on/off valve and a lockshield valve, controlling the rate at which water leaves the radiator. Of the top two, one is merely plugged, while the other houses the bleed vent.

Both valves are fitted to the radiator using tail pieces (often supplied with the valve). Wrap their threads in PTFE tape to ensure a watertight join. Tape is also needed around the thread of the radiator plug, but here you may have trouble tightening up, since the plug will normally have only a square or octagonal recess by which it can be gripped. A 'tommy bar' is needed here. However, before going to the expense of buying one, try using a large screwdriver.

Finally, the bleed vent. How you fit this depends on its design. If the part turned by the vent key is encased in an outer sleeve, bind the sleeve's thread with PTFE tape, then screw it into place with a spanner. If you have a one-piece vent, the whole of which screws in and out of the radiator, use the vent key to drive it home. Do not use tape or jointing compound on its thread.

Hanging the radiator

You can now hang the radiator. It hooks on special brackets screwed to the wall, but make sure the wall fixings are firm – a full radiator is heavy. In solid masonry, ensure wall plugs expand in the body of the wall; not in the plaster. On stud partition and lath-and-plaster clad walls, don't use cavity fixings. Screw into the timber studs or into battens screwed to bridge two or more studs.

Care is also needed when positioning the brackets, if the radiator is to be in the right place. Measure the distance between the centres of the fixing lugs on the back of the radiator, and the distance between the lugs and the radiator's top and bottom edge. From these you can work out where the brackets should go for any given radiator position, and so long as you check that the brackets are vertical all should be well.

Finally, connect the feed and return branch pipes to the radiator valves. This is normally done using compression joints. Connect the feed pipe to the on/off valve and the lockshield valve to the return.

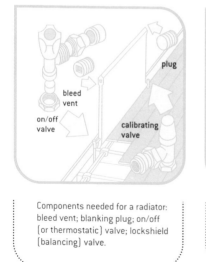

Components needed for a radiator: bleed vent; blanking plug; on/off (or thermostatic) valve; lockshield (balancing) valve.

Lift the radiator on to the two level brackets. Plastic sleeves pushed on to the bracket lugs will prevent expansion noise.

How to clear blockages

It is much better to treat a sluggish waste outlet before it becomes completely blocked and a real emergency. Scalding water is particularly effective against a build-up of grease, at a kitchen sink, but the blockage may also be caused by a small object which lodges itself across the pipe and other small particles of waste become trapped and very quickly build up into a fairly solid blockage. An ordinary rubber plunger and drain auger are the most effective tools to use for freeing a blocked waste outlet in hand basins and sinks.

Using a plunger

Begin by plugging the overflow opening with soft cloth and allowing enough water in the basin to cover the plunger cup. Coat the rim of the cup with petroleum jelly and place in centrally over the plughole. Without breaking the seal between the sink and the cup, pump vigorously up and down. Then quickly release the plunger, when the blockage should be free. If not, then use the drain auger, or try cleaning the trap.

Using a drain auger

Should the plunger not work, then try the drain auger (snake). This is a very flexible metal coil that can be fed through the pipes until it reaches the blockage. The drain auger can be inserted into the basin if the strainer can be removed from the plug recess.

Feed the auger into the waste by winding the handle clockwise. When you reach the blockage, move the auger backwards and forwards slowly while still winding, then slowly withdraw it, winding in the same direction.

Clearing the trap

Most modern sinks and basins have a removable bottle trap that forms part of the U-bend, and is situated directly below the plug outlet. Place a container beneath the U-bend to catch the water in the trap. Unscrew the bottom half and probe (using a small piece of wood) inside and around the inner pipe where waste collects. Clean and replace the trap. Turn on the water to check that it is now free flowing.

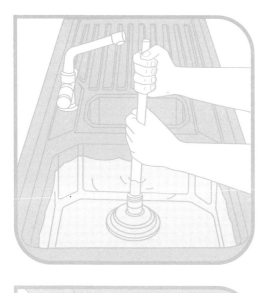

Pump the plunger rapidly up and down for about 10 strokes; then quickly jerk the plunger away to remove the blockage.

Unscrew the lower half of the bottle trap over a container and, using a small length of wood, probe inside to release the blockage. Clean the trap and reassemble.

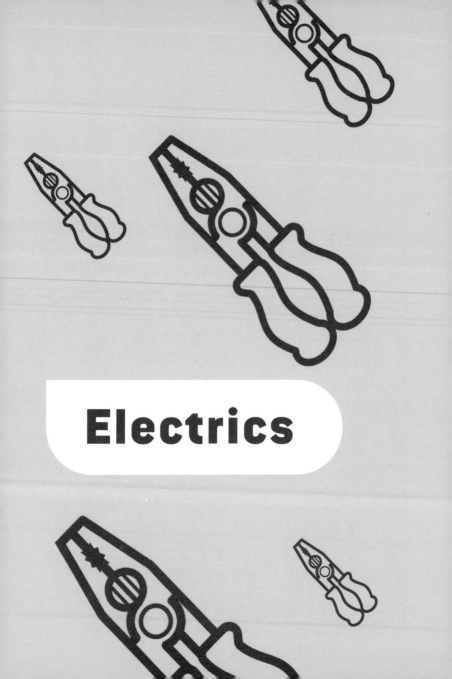

Electrics

Electricity is very dangerous. If you are inexperienced, tampering with your household electrics is very unwise and could be fatal. Modern building regulations recommend that most electrical work should be carried out by a certified electrician. However, there is some very basic electrical work that can be tackled by the DIY enthusiast – including mending a fuse, wiring a plug and installing a socket. But always ensure that you switch off the fuse box before doing anything else. And if in any doubt call in an expert.

How to deal with electrical emergencies

In the previous chapter we assessed four common plumbing emergencies. Electrical emergencies are potentially more serious. Simply being without power is highly inconvenient, but electrical fires or electrical shocks are life threatening. Study the advice contained here and learn how to cope with three common electrical emergencies.

FUSE BOX WARNING

The main on-off switch on your fuse box (consumer unit) disconnects only the fuses or miniature circuit breakers (MCBs) and the cables leading out from it to the household circuits. It does NOT disconnect the cables entering via the meter from the service cable. Do not tamper with these cables. They are always live at mains voltage.

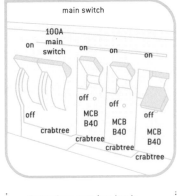

Know where your fuse box is located and how to use it.

Fire in an appliance

1

If a plug-in appliance catches fire, switch the appliance off at the socket outlet and pull out the plug.

2

If a fixed appliance with no plug is on fire, turn it off at the wall switch if you can, or at the main switch on the fuse box.

3

Do not use water on an electrical fire. Smother the fire with a rug or blanket, or use a dry-powder fire extinguisher.

4

Get the appliance checked (and repaired if necessary) by an expert before you use it again. Otherwise, replace it.

Smell of overheating

1

If you smell burning from an appliance, turn off the switch at the socket and pull out the plug. If it is a fixed appliance with no plug, turn off its wall switch or the main switch at the consumer unit. Turn off the appliance switch and call an expert. An electrician can check flex connections, renew them if necessary and, if they are sound, check the appliance. If the appliance is under guarantee, call the supplier.

2

If the smell comes from a socket outlet or a plug, turn off the main switch at the consumer unit. If the plug is hot, let it cool before unplugging it. Then check its connections, including the fuse contacts, and examine the flex for damage. Replace the plug if necessary (page 170). If the socket is hot, call an electrician.

No electricity

1

If power throughout your house fails and neighbouring houses are also without power, there is a mains supply failure. Report it to the 24-hour emergency number under 'Electricity' in the phone book.

2

If your system is protected by a whole-house residual current device (RCD), check whether it has switched itself off. Try to switch it on again if it has.

3

If it will not switch on, the fault that tripped it off is still present on the system. Call an electrician to track it down and rectify it.

4

If you do not have an RCD and your house is the only one without power, there may be a fault in your supply cable, or your main supply fuse may have blown. Do not touch it. Report the power failure as above.

How to mend a fuse

The fuse box is essentially the circuit breaker of your home. If you notice power has failed, for instance a light, it is likely that the light bulb has broken. In this instance, a fuse interrupts excessive current (blows) in order to protect the electrical system from further damage. To restore power you will need to change the fuse.

Fuse boxes are fitted with either fuse wire or cartridge fuses. If you still have the former, keep spare fuses or fuse wire to hand for instant repairs if a fuse 'blows'.

Replacing fuse wire

1

Turn off the main on/off switch on the consumer unit. Remove or open the cover over the fuse carriers.

2

Pull out each fuse carrier (see opposite for types of carrier) in turn to find out which has blown. Scorch marks often show this, or a break in the wire.

3

If a power circuit is affected, switch off and unplug all the appliances on the circuit. If it is a lighting circuit, turn off all the light switches. If you do not switch everything off, the mended fuse is likely to blow again immediately you turn the mains back on.

4

Loosen the two terminal screws and remove any pieces of old wire. Cut a new piece of fuse wire of the correct amp rating, long enough to cross the carrier and go round both screws.

5

Wind the wire clockwise round one screw and tighten the screw. Pass the wire across the bridge or thread it through the holder. If you are unsure about how the wire runs in the carrier, examine one of the intact fuses.

6

Wind the wire clockwise round the second screw. Make sure there is a little slack in the wire so that it will not snap, and then tighten the screw.

7

Replace the fuse carrier in the consumer unit. Close the cover and restore the power by turning on the main switch. Then check the circuit (see right).

Replacing a cartridge fuse

1

Turn off the main switch on the consumer unit. If you have cartridge fuses, you will need a fuse tester that will tell you if a cartridge fuse has blown.

2

Find out which fuse has blown: take out each fuse carrier in turn so you can test the cartridge.

3

Prise the cartridge gently from the clamps. Some carriers are in two halves and the screw holding them together has to be removed to give access to the cartridge.

4

Remove one carrier at a time; test its cartridge with a fuse tester, and replace it before removing the next one for testing. When you have traced the blown fuse, replace the cartridge with a new one of the amp rating shown on the carrier.

5

As with a rewirable fuse, switch off all appliances or lights on the affected circuit. Replace the fuse carrier, close the box and turn on the main switch. Then check the circuit.

Bridged fuse – The wire runs from one terminal to the other over a plug of white arc-damping material. The carrier is ceramic.

Protected fuse – Between the terminals the wire runs through a porcelain arc-damping tube. The carrier is tough plastic.

Fuse between humps – The unprotected wire passes round humps between one terminal and the other. The carrier is ceramic.

retaining screw

fuse carrier

clamp

How to extend a flex

Flexes are the cables that attach to an electrical appliance at one end and a plug at the other. In some cases, where the cable isn't long enough to reach the power source at the wall – and an extension cable is deemed unsightly – you might want to join the cable to another longer piece. This is how you do it.

WARNING

Never join lengths of flex by twisting together the cores and binding the join with insulating tape. It may overheat and start a fire.

YOU WILL NEED

Tools Screwdrivers; sharp knife; wire cutters and strippers; pliers.

Materials Flex connector; length of flex fitted with a plug.

If you have to extend a flex, use a one-piece connector to make a permanent joint, or use a two-part connector if you want to be able to separate the joint. This must have three pins for connecting appliances that use three-core flex. Two-pin connectors are used mainly for connecting double-insulated garden power tools to extension leads.

1

Unscrew the connector cover and remove it. Prepare the ends of both flexes for connection by stripping back the insulating sheath and checking that the cores will be long enough to reach their brass terminals. Strip about 15mm (½ in) of coloured insulation from each core.

2

Lift out the brass barrel terminals and loosen all the terminal screws.

3

Push the cores into the terminals so that they match – brown to brown in one terminal, green-and-yellow to green-and-yellow in the second, and blue to blue in the third. Tighten all the terminal screws.

4

Loosen one screw and remove the other from each cord grip so that you can swing the bar aside.

5

Fit the brass barrel terminals in their slots and position each flex sheath beneath its cord grip.

6

Replace the cord grip screws and tighten them to grip the flex sheaths securely (opposite left). Fit and screw on the cover.

ELECTRIC SHOCK

If you get a minor shock from an electrical appliance, a plug or other wiring accessory, stop using it immediately. Get a repair expert to check the appliance for earth safety, and replace damaged plugs and wiring accessories as soon as possible. Use PVC insulating tape to make a temporary repair.

If someone receives a major shock, DO NOT touch bare flesh while the person is in contact with the source of the current. If you do, the current will pass through you as well, giving you an electric shock.

FAULT FINDING

If one appliance fails to work, unplug it and check its plug, fuse and flex; renew them as necessary. If the appliance still fails to work, plug it in a different socket outlet to test it. If it works, the problem is with the original socket; if not, take the appliance to an expert for repair.

How to wire a plug

The three-pin plug is a vital link between an electrical appliance and its power supply from a socket outlet, and if it is to do its job properly it must be correctly and securely wired up. In addition, if its fuse is going to protect the appliance in the event of a fault, it must be of the correct rating for the appliance concerned.

1

To connect an appliance flex to a plug, the first step is to open the plug by unscrewing its top, and to lay the flex over its base so you can see how long the cores have to be to reach from the cord grip to the furthest terminal.

2

Cut away the outer sheathing of the flex to expose the cores, taking care not to nick their insulation as you do so. Again lay the flex in place, checking that the cores will reach their terminals, and trim to length any that are overlong.

3

Next, strip off about 12mm (½ in) of insulation from each core, and twist the stranded conductors tightly together. Use wire strippers for this so that you don't cut through any of the strands.

4

Then attach them to their terminals. With the plug interior facing you, you should connect the live (brown or red) core to the bottom right-hand terminal – the one to which the plug fuse is connected. The neutral (blue or black) core goes to the bottom left terminal, while the earth core (green-and-yellow or plain green) is linked to the top terminal furthest from the cord grip. With some appliances two-core flex without an earth core is used; in this case there is no connection to the earth terminal.

5

Some plugs have pillar terminals, with the core secured in a hole in the pin by a small screw. Double over the bared flex end to increase the contact area before inserting it in the hole. Others have stud terminals, with the core secured round a

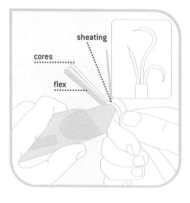

sheating

cores

flex

Stripping off the outer sheathing of the flex; cut round carefully, making sure not to damage the insulation on the cores.

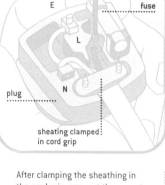

E

fuse

L

plug

N

sheating clamped in cord grip

After clamping the sheathing in the cord grip, connect the cores to the terminals, making sure there are no stray strands of wire.

threaded stud by a screw-down washer and nut. Here, wind the core clockwise round the stud before tightening down the washer.

6

Finally, lay the cores in their channels and secure the outer sheathing of the flex in the cord grip.

7

Fit a fuse of the correct rating – 3A for appliances rated at up to 720 watts, a 13A one otherwise – and close the plug securely.

Fuse trouble

If one of your household appliances stops working – be it a kettle or vacuum cleaner – do not immediately throw the item away. It is possible that the plug fuse has blown. Fuses are readily available from all hardware stores and, as shown, are very easy to fit.

How to change a plug socket

You might wish to change a plug socket for three reasons: either the socket appears to be faulty; you wish to change the style, from plastic to chrome, for instance; or you wish to change the size, perhaps from a single to a double. Providing you don't wish to change the location of the socket in the wall, this is a task that you can complete without calling in a qualified electrician.

Remove the face plate and examine (but do not touch) the exposed wires.

Check the wires are secure and not trapped and then screw the new socket into position.

1

First turn off the main switch at the consumer box and remove or switch off the relevant fuse as marked. It is important to always check that the socket (single or double) is dead – this can be done with an appliance you know to be working.

2

Using an electrician's screwdriver, undo the two screws holding the face plate and gently ease the socket away from the wall. Now loosen the three terminal screws to release the wires from the socket. Check for signs of damage. If in doubt consult an electrician.

3

Now make a note of which wires are connected to each terminal. This will remain the same for your new socket.

4

If there is enough slack from the existing wires, a surface box can be fitted. Simply position the new box centrally over the existing hole and mark through for wall fixings. Note where the cables run in the wall, as care must be taken when drilling.

5

Pass the cables through the hole in the new box and then screw into place. Now connect up the double socket as previously noted in step 3. Slide a green-and-yellow earth sleeve over any bare earth wires.

6

Check each group of wires are secure and not trapped before screwing the socket fully into the mounting box. This would require the fitting of a new metal wall box if this is the type of socket you require.

Cosmetic changes

If you do not like the appearance of your wall sockets you can change to an alternative style. Choose from white plastic, brushed silver and chrome. You can also opt for face plates that are either raised or sit flush to the wall. Similiar choices are available for light switches and telephone points.

How to install a ceiling canopy

Replacing or installing a ceiling canopy is another quick and simple job that is within the capabilities of an enthusiastic do-it-yourselfer. All you really need is a screwdriver and a voltage tester.

1

First switch off the power at the appropriate circuit breaker to isolate the circuit.

2

Remove the existing light and fitting and the canopy and, using a voltage tester, double check to make sure that the terminals are quite dead.

3

After removing the canopy, it is important to identify the wires and, perhaps, make a careful diagram of the way the wires are connected, so that you can confidently rewire the new ceiling junction box in the same way.

4

Disconnect the wires from the terminal canopy. If the existing junction box is unstable, you might want to nail a mounting board between the joists above the box position and drill a hole through for the cable.

5

Screw the backplate in position and bring the cable through.

6

Make sure the ends of the wires are sound and clean, then fix them to the terminals carefully, following your diagram.

7

Having made sure the terminals are soundly connected, thread the new canopy up the cable and screw into the existing junction box.

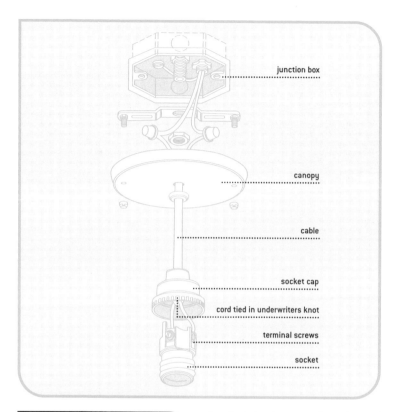

junction box

canopy

cable

socket cap

cord tied in underwriters knot

terminal screws

socket

Replacing a halogen

Gently squeeze together the two ends of the circlip just visible around the inner edge of the fitting. Remove the circlip and the bulb will be released. Pull the bulb away from the plug at the end of the wire and attach the new bulb. Push it into the ceiling recess and replace the circlip.

Replacing the canopy of a pendant light and the cable (if needed). When replacing the cable, make sure it is reinforced pendant cable capable of carrying the additional weight of a glass or acrylic shade, if used.

Miscellaneous

You might well now consider yourself an expert in the areas of painting and decorating, basic electrics, plumbing, and inside and outside maintenance, but what about problems of damp and heat retention? This final chapter reveals all.

How to cure rising damp

Rising damp is caused when moisture from the ground on which the house stands is soaked up into its masonry walls. The dampness can rise to a height of 900mm (36in) or so above skirting board level, causing unsightly staining of the plaster and the decorations and also an unpleasant smell in the affected rooms. It can also cause rot in floor timbers, door frames and skirting boards.

Causes

The dampness can be caused by a failure in the dampproof course that is built into the walls — a particularly common fault in older properties where slates or engineering bricks were used to form the damp course. It can also result from the damp course being bridged in some way — by an adjoining wall, by garden soil being banked up against the wall, or by steps, paths or other outdoor features being built alongside the wall. The latter need not be above the damp course level to cause rising damp; heavy rain can splash back off these surfaces to soak the wall above. Even a coat of rendering on the exterior wall can suck moisture up above the damp course if it extends down over it.

Solving rising damp

If you have rising damp, check whether any of the above-mentioned problems are present. Remove any you find and see whether the wall shows signs of drying out. Only if the problem persists should you call in a professional firm of dampproofing specialists for their advice on the best solution to the problem.

! ROGUE TRADERS

Beware of specialist damp prevention companies selling expensive cures for rising damp — often in the form of a series of injections of resin into your exterior walls. These companies sometimes misdiagnose penetrating damp as rising damp. In these instances you will waste your money.

fractured dpc

Common causes of rising damp include cracks in old damp courses, paths and steps built against the wall above (or close to) the level of the damp course, adjoining garden or outbuilding walls built against the house wall without a vertical damp course, rendering covering the damp course, or garden soil built up against the house wall above the damp course.

soil built up above dpc

How to cure penetrating damp

Penetrating damp can usually be traced back to an obvious fault like a leaking pipe. Repair the cause and the dampness should disappear. However, there is one form of penetrating damp that's harder to identify and cure, and that is dampness soaking through the very fabric of exterior walls.

Pointing pointers

Check the mortar pointing between bricks. If this has crumbled or fallen out, it is easier for rain to enter the wall.

Start by hacking out old, unsound pointing with a small cold chisel and club hammer, aiming to cut back to a depth of about 10mm (½ in). Brush out any loose debris, then splash in clean water to help the new mortar to stick.

Use a 1:4 mix of cement and sharp sand; for small areas buy this dry ready-mixed in bags. Make a 'hawk' from a square of chipboard with a dowel handle nailed in the centre and use to hold a small amount of mortar close to the wall. Mould the mortar into a pudding shape then cut off a sausage-shape on the back of a small pointing trowel. Press this firmly into place between bricks, then continue until you've covered about 1sq m (1sq yd), then go back and apply a pointing profile to match the surrounding wall.

There are three main pointing profiles designed to reflect rainwater from the surface of the wall:

Flush pointing Smooth the mortar level with the face of the wall, using a wad of sacking or coarse hessian. Use for sheltered walls only, or where the surface is to be painted.

Rounded pointing (see opposite, top) Indent the mortar using a length of 10mm (½ in) diameter dowel or plastic tube to give it a delicate half-round profile.

Weather-struck pointing (see opposite, bottom) For exposed walls. Use the trowel to shape the mortar into a neat sloping bevel: use a long, straight timber batten held against the wall to steady your hand as you work.

With either pointing profile, tackle the verticals before the horizontals.

Wall faults

With the pointing completed, check the masonry. Moisture penetrating a cracked brick may freeze in winter, then expand and literally 'blow' the face off the brick: this 'spalling' allows moisture to soak in to the extent that rain often appears to pour through the wall. Cracked or spalled bricks should be hacked out with a cold chisel and club hammer and replaced. Chop around the brick to free it or drill into it many times with a large masonry bit, then attack the brick and remove the fragments.

If bricks aren't badly spalled, make good with a little car body filler with brick dust sprinkled on to match the brickwork.
Replacing a brick To replace a brick, try to find a second-hand one to match the rest of the wall. Clean up the inside of the hole, dampen it, then line the bottom and one end with a stiff mortar mix.

Butter the top and one end of the replacement brick by scraping the mortar off the trowel. Form a wedge-shape and furrow the mortar to aid suction. Insert the brick in the hole, buttered end to clean end, tap in place and point the joints.

Filling Where the damage is less extensive, rake out cracks and small holes, undercutting the surrounding sound material to form a ledge for the filler material to grip to. Fill with a 1:5 mix of cement and sharp sand, or a proprietary exterior filler.

Blown render 'Blown' or blistered areas of render that have come away from the brickwork should be cut away with a hammer and chisel and filled with mortar to within about 25mm (1in) of the surface. Allow this to stiffen, then scratch the surface with the edge of a steel float or trowel to provide a key for the finishing coat. This can consist of plain mortar or mortar mixed with fine aggregate – depending on the texture of the original; try to match the surrounding surface. Once applied, saw it off level with the surrounding wall by drawing a straight-edged timber batten across the surface.

How to fit an extractor fan

Extractor fans are very useful in bathrooms for removing the build up of damp air and helping to avoid condensation. You will need a specialist drill bit to bore a hole large enough to accommodate the fan. That aside, this is a fairly straightforward task.

Drill

Most designs of extractor fan will require a circular hole to be cut through the house wall. The best tool to use for this is a heavy-duty electric drill fitted with a core drill bit, both of which you can hire. These will cut a hole of exactly the right size. Make holes in both leaves of a cavity wall and fit the sleeve supplied with the extractor fan. Keep as much debris as possible out of the wall cavity, since this could bridge the cavity and lead to damp problems. Once the sleeve for the fan is in place, make good the brickwork and plaster.

Fitting the fan is easy – drill holes for wall plugs to take the fan on the inside wall, and fit the outlet on the outer wall.

Wiring

An extractor fan needs to be wired up via a fused connection unit to the nearest power supply circuit. If you are not sure how to do this, employ a qualified electrician to do the job. In a bathroom or shower room, with no opening window, a fan is a compulsory requirement and it must be wired via the light switch so that it comes on with the light and remains on for 15 minutes after the light is turned off.

Once the wiring is complete, check that the extractor functions correctly. Then fix the cover of the unit on with screws.

How to repair an airbrick

Airbricks are vital, providing ventilation in any home. Broken airbricks can cause problems, since they will provide access for vermin under the ground floor, where they may multiply and find their way into other parts of the house. You will need to remove the old airbrick and replace it with one of the same style and size.

With a solid wall, it is unlikely that the opening will be lined. In more modern houses, the cavity between the inner and outer skins of the brickwork should be sealed to prevent dissipation of air into the cavity. You can do this with clay ducts or slates.

Fitting airbricks

Replacement airbricks, which are made from clay, cast iron or cast aluminium, must fit flush with the surface of the wall and be bedded in with cement mortar.

Remember to keep airbricks clear. They must never be blocked up, since their purpose is to ventilate timber floors and prevent them from getting damp and being attacked by rot.

Types of airbrick

Airbricks are essential for providing ventilation to the voids beneath timber floors, and so helping to prevent rot attacking the floor timbers. Terracotta bricks are installed with a matching

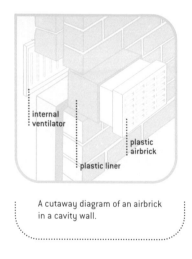

internal ventilator

plastic airbrick

plastic liner

A cutaway diagram of an airbrick in a cavity wall.

cavity sleeve, while plastic types slide within a plastic sleeve to cope with a range of wall thicknesses. Both come in a range of sizes.

How to cure woodworm and rot

Timber floors in a house have two natural enemies — woodworm and rot. Both will attack where the right conditions exist. It is a classical case of prevention being better than cure, since the upheaval and cost of remedying either can be considerable.

Woodworm

You are more likely to recognise the signs of woodworm than the beetle itself, since the surface of attacked timber is punctured by tiny holes about 2mm (¹/₁₀in) in diameter. One beetle species differs in that it leaves irregular oval slits up to 9mm (¹/₃in) wide on the surface.

Curing woodworm

Under the floorboards the timber will probably be covered with dirt and dust. This must be removed to enable you to carry out a thorough inspection and treatment. Where there is severe damage to the joists, you will have to have them strengthened or replaced, so expert advice could be essential.

When it comes to treating affected areas, insecticide is available in cans, which you can either spray or brush on. With some cans and aerosols a special plastic nozzle is supplied to enable you to inject the fluid more easily into the flight holes — for example, in furniture.

Although the treatment can be carried out at any time of year, the best period is in the summer, when windows and doors can be left open. Woodworm fluid leaves a pungent odour, which is very strong for the first couple of days and will still be evident several weeks later.

Wood rot

Wood rot is usually categorised as either 'wet' or 'dry', which is confusing since dampness causes them both. They are both fungi and there are various species of each type. Wet rot confines itself to damp wood, whereas dry rot can spread itself from wet to dry material. So obviously the best way to discourage rot is to guard against damp penetration.

Recognising wet rot

Wet rot is the name given to the cellar fungus *Coniophora cerebella*. This is found in floors and also causes decay on fence posts, wooden sheds, windowsills and other outdoor timbers.

Mercifully, wet rot does not produce well-developed conducting strands and so it will not penetrate brick walls. Bathrooms, kitchens and cellars are typical places to find it.

Curing wet rot

First locate the source of the damp and cure it. Then allow the wood to dry out, since this will make the fungus inactive. Cut back infected timber to sound material and replace it with new timber. Smaller areas can be repaired with a wood filler. Finally, treat new timber and all surrounding areas of wood with preservative.

Recognising dry rot

The dry rot fungus *Merulius lacrymans* flourishes under conditions of bad ventilation and high humidity. It is more efficient at destroying wood than any other fungus and, once established, can even spread to wood that would normally be too dry to be attacked.

Early on, dry rot is a fluffy white growth, which soon resembles thick cotton wool. The wood later appears to be coated with grey matted strands, behind which the fungus forms thicker strands capable of transporting moisture from one part of the timber to another. This creates the ideal conditions for the spread of the fungus to new sites.

Curing dry rot

Remove all affected timber and burn it immediately. Examine any surrounding plaster to determine the full extent of the attack and make sure you cut back the problem area to about 1m (3ft) beyond the farthest sign of trouble. Use a blowlamp to kill surface spores and strands on brickwork and the subfloor.

Having sterilised all surfaces, paint the brickwork, subfloor and all timber within about 2m (6ft) of the attack with dry rot fluid. Apply the recommended number of coats.

You can treat woodworm infestation yourself, using hired spraying equipment and protective clothing, but the chemicals needed are unpleasant and potentially dangerous to inhale. So, for all but small-scale attacks, it is preferable to call in a professional firm who will treat the attack thoroughly and also issue a guarantee against fresh attacks.

How to seal doors and windows

Cold air and moisture will always find a way to penetrate your home, so in milder weather closely examine your doors and windows for any gaps. Use either frame sealants or foam filler to remedy the problem. That way you'll keep damp and cold air out and warm air in during winter.

Using frame sealants

Damp patches on the walls around a window frame indicate that rain is seeping through the gap between the frame and the wall. These gaps are sealed when the windows are installed, but often the old caulking material used fails and eventually falls out.

The problem with using a normal cellulose filler or mortar mix to fill these gaps is that both set rigid. Throughout the year the gap opens and closes due to natural seasonal movement of the structure. Since the filling material is rigid, it eventually cracks and falls out.

In this situation you must use a mastic sealant, which will remain flexible. There are sealants available for different situations and you need to buy one specifically for dealing with window frames. They are supplied in a cartridge and used with a special applicator gun, which you have to buy separately. Colours include white, grey and brown and the mastic can be painted over if desired.

First you must prepare the affected area, brushing down the gap and surround to remove dirt and debris. Then apply the sealant as a continuous bead along the length of the gap.

Using expanding foam fillers

Wherever pipes, cables or flues penetrate walls or roofs, there is a potential damp problem lurking. An ideal quick solution for sealing such areas is available with expanding foam fillers. Supplied in an aerosol, these fillers are simply sprayed on, then left to expand and fill any shape of hole. They will stick to virtually any surface and can be cut or shaped with a knife or hacksaw when dry. However, they can be very sticky to the touch, so always wear protective gloves when using them.

Filler foams are ideal for sealing irregular gaps in awkward places, the kind of areas that would otherwise be inadequately plugged or left exposed to allow damp to gain a hold.

Left: Expanding foam fillers are ideal for filling irregular gaps. Trim them to shape once they have hardened, and protect them with a layer of exterior filler or mortar.

Below: Mastics are used to seal a wide range of small gaps on house exteriors. Their surface quickly skins over, allowing them to be painted if necessary, but the body of the mastic bead stays flexible and so copes with any structural movement that may occur.

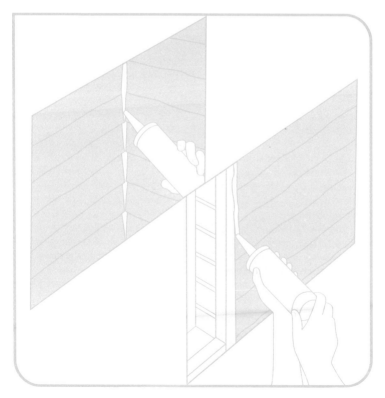

TIP 95

How to insulate a loft

There are two DIY ways to insulate the loft. You can use rolls (of mineral wool or glass fibre) or loosefill material (vermiculite, a lightweight expanded mineral, or polystyrene granules) sold in bags. Though the two methods are comparable in terms of cost and efficiency, glass fibre blanket is the more popular.

Insulation material

Blanket materials are generally easier to handle than loosefill types, unless your loft contains a lot of obstructions or has irregular joist spacings. The rolls are normally 400mm (16in) wide to match the standard joist spacing and common thicknesses are 100mm (4in) and 150mm (6in). Choose the former if there is already some insulation and simply lay it on top of the existing material. If there is none at all, then you should use the thicker blanket.

Insulation thickness

It is worth checking the thickness of any existing insulation if you move to another house. If it has been built in the mid-sixties, it could well have an inadequate layer, since 25mm (1in) was the thickness stipulated by the Building Regulations at that time. It is also worth remembering that over a period of years blanket insulation can naturally compress and shrink in thickness.

Ventilation

Ventilation is essential in any loft to prevent condensation forming in the winter months and causing rot in the roof timbers, as well as dampening the insulation and thus making it ineffective. This means providing extra ventilation openings at the eaves by drilling holes in the soffit boards or by installing additional airbricks in gable walls. Never pack the eaves with insulation, since this will tend to cut off the airflow. Special eaves vents are available which fit between the joists and prevent the insulation material from restricting the flow of air. In an unboarded roof, the gaps between the tiles will usually ensure sufficient ventilation.

One area that should not be insulated is the loft floor below the cold water tank. Any warmth rising from the room underneath will be beneficial in helping to prevent winter freeze-ups. But you must insulate the top of the trap door into the loft.

Lagging pipes

Thorough insulation makes it even more vital to lag all the plumbing pipes and the cold water tank, since the loft is going to be even colder in winter. The pipes can be wrapped in glass fibre bandage or moulded foam tubes. Moulded foam tubes have a slit along one side, which enables you to push them over the pipes. You then tape them to keep the insulation securely in place. Pay special attention to bends, making sure you do not leave any pipes exposed.

The tank can be wrapped in a purpose-made insulating jacket or glass fibre. Equally, it can be boxed in with 25mm (1in) thick slabs of polystyrene. The tank must have a 'lid' on it to prevent the possibility of the water freezing and to ensure that spiders, birds and any other creatures that have found their way into the loft do not drop into the water and contaminate it.

insulation on hatch cover

Remember to insulate above the loft hatch, to leave clearance at the eaves for ventilation via soffit vents, and to insulate any water tanks and pipes in the loft space. Leave the ceiling beneath the water tanks uninsulated.

Heat loss

Older properties will still have a hot water cylinder – probably situated in the airing cupboard. A purpose-made insulating jacket is by far the best to use and you will recover its cost in a couple of months – just one indication of what an uninsulated cylinder will cost you!

roll insulation

Loft floors can be insulated by laying glass fibre blankets or semi-rigid insulation batts between the ceiling joists, or by spreading a loose-fill insulating material such as vermiculite to a uniform depth.

How to insulate a wall

Wall insulation, alongside loft insulation, is one of the best methods for retaining heat in your home. There are two main methods to use. Here's how you do it.

If the wall to be insulated has no switches, doors or windows, then the job is very straightforward. However, where these obstacles exist, then the work is much more tricky. Switches and sockets will have to be repositioned on the new wall surface and architraves and skirting removed and refixed. You will also have to cut round window and door frames.

Thermal board

If the wall is flat, you can use vapour-check thermal board and stick it directly to the surface with a special adhesive and secondary nail fixing. Thermal board is a standard plasterboard bonded to a backing of expanded polystyrene with a polythene film sandwiched in between.

Plasterboard

Where the wall is uneven, you will have to put up a framework of battens to provide a level surface on which you can then fix standard (general-purpose) plasterboard. This has an ivory coloured side over which you can paint or paper directly.

Plasterboard can be cut quite easily using either a fine-tooth tenon saw or a sharp knife, which is more convenient and less messy. Holes and other cut-outs, to accept light switches and sockets, for example, can easily be made with a pad saw or power jigsaw.

When working with plasterboard, bear in mind that it is very cumbersome and awkward to handle and you should have two people to carry it.

Having lined the walls, you then have to replace the skirting boards and reposition any sockets and switches. Your new wall is then ready for decorating.

! CAVITY WALLS

If your house has cavity walls, then the simplest method of insulation is to have the cavity filled. The process is not a DIY job and should be tackled by a specialist company.

How to insulate flooring

A solid floor does not normally have to be insulated, since a straightforward floorcovering is sufficient to keep it warm underfoot. A timber floor, however, is a quite different matter, since it is essential that some air flows constantly beneath it to keep the joists and boards free from damp.

In extreme cases, such as in a very severe climate or where the room is over a garage and therefore particularly cold, you may have to take more severe measures.

If there is enough space under a suspended timber floor to crawl into, it is quite easy to fix insulation between the joists under the floorboards. You can use rigid polystyrene, cutting it into strips and resting it on nails driven into the sides of the joists. Alternatively, you

can suspend lengths of insulation blanket between the joists, using garden netting stapled to the joists as support. If there is only a narrow space under the floor, you will have to lift all the floorboards first. This will inevitably cause a lot more disruption within the room concerned.

This method is the best way of insulating rooms above cold, ground-floor areas such as integral garages.

floorboards

polystyrene insulation

battens pinned to joist sides

How to draughtproof

A house that has not been draughtproofed can never be kept really warm and comfortable. And there is nothing more unpleasant than icy cold draughts whistling around you on a cold winter's night. Although such work can be time consuming, it is not expensive. In fact, under normal circumstances you can look forward to recovering the cost of adding full draughtproofing to a house within three years.

When you are working out what draughtproofing materials you need, doors and windows should be top of the list. But do not forget other areas such as letterboxes, keyholes and, of course, those major culprits such as floors and any disused chimney flues.

Frame insulation

For window and door frames, you will find there is a variety of different materials to choose from, the simplest and cheapest being self-adhesive foam and brush strips. Supplied in rolls, they are simply stuck to the appropriate place on the frame so that the door or window closes against them.

Other, more expensive devices include V-shaped lengths of plastic, phosphor bronze or aluminium, which are pinned to the frame. The door or window then compresses the V shape when shut, sealing out any draughts.

Door bottoms

For the bottom of doors you also have several options. All are simple and quick to fit, although some are more sophisticated and effective than others.

The basic type is a strip of wood, metal or plastic housing a rubber, brush or plastic insert that grazes along the floorcovering when the door is closed. Cut it to length and pin or screw it to the door. If you have the type with pre-drilled screw holes, you should trim where necessary from both ends to ensure the remaining holes are evenly spaced. You can drill new holes in the strip if you have to.

There is also a rise-and-fall excluder, which will lift above the floorcovering as the door opens and then fall back into place when the door is closed. Another type comes in two parts, one fitting to the bottom of the door and the other to the threshold. The two parts interlock when you close the door.

Draughtproof sliding sash windows by pinning on proprietary excluders down the edges and across the meeting rail. Check that the window still slides freely.

Use self-adhesive foam excluders to draughtproof casement windows and doors, sticking the strips into the rebates so they are fully compressed when the window or door is closed.

How to install double glazing

Exactly how much heat double glazing will save is debatable; much depends on the number and size of the windows in the house. It is generally estimated that about 10–15 per cent of heat goes out through the windows of the average house and that this can be halved with an efficient, well-installed system.

Double glazing companies will refit entirely new windows in your home, often at great expense. However, a cheaper method is to fit secondary glazing, which is available as a DIY kit. The advantage here is that the existing windows remain in place so that the outside appearance of the house is unaltered. This type is fixed on the inside, either to the existing window frames or to the surrounding walls of the window reveal.

Clear film

The simplest and cheapest DIY system uses a clear, durable sheet of film, which you can fix in minutes. Cut the film to the overall size of the window, with an allowance of 50mm (2in) all round. Then fix double-sided adhesive tape around the frame and secure the film to this around the edges. Finally, heat the film with a hair dryer to remove all the wrinkles. Trim off any excess film with a sharp knife.

Magnetic plastic

The slightly more sophisticated magnetic system uses clear rigid plastic instead of glass, but still requires no clips, screws or other similar fixings. Cut the plastic sheet to the size of the window frame and then fix steel strip around the outside of the frame. Apply the matching magnetic strip around the perimeter of the plastic sheet and position this so that the two strips meet. The magnetism will hold the glazing in place.

Double glazing kits

Conventional double glazing kits are similar in principle and vary only in detail. A framework of PVC or aluminium accepts the glass and this assembly is then fixed either direct to the existing window frame or to the walls of the window reveals. The glazing panels can be fixed, hinged or sliding. Hinged or sliding panels will give access to any windows you may want to open, whether side or top hung.

Assembling and fitting

There is generally no problem in fixing the double glazing frames to an existing timber-framed window; metal frames, however, are more awkward. If the system you choose is suitable for fixing to metal, then you will need either self-tapping screws or you will have to install a secondary timber frame around the window on which to mount the system.

It is a relatively straightforward job mounting the double glazing directly on to the window frame. Fixing it into the window reveal can be quite difficult, since reveals are rarely exactly square. But it is essential to ensure your frame is perfectly square if the panels are to slide, hinge or close properly.

Check the existing handles and stays. If they project too far, they will prevent you fitting your system to the window frame. If you do not want to fix the glazing to the window reveal, then you will have to change them.

The different systems are all assembled and fitted in a similar way. However, if you want a hinged system, you will need to construct a timber framework on which to mount the secondary glazing and then hang the whole assembly on brackets.

Provided both the existing window frame and the double glazing you have to put up are both well sealed, the problem of condensation between the two layers of glass can largely be avoided. It is advisable to install your system on a day when the air in the room is cold and dry. If damp air is trapped inside the cavity, inter-pane misting will be a constant problem in the future.

Start fitting sliding secondary glazing by cutting the side tracks to length. Then screw the side (top), top and bottom tracks to the frame or reveal. Next, measure and cut to length the channels that frame the glass, and fit them to the panes (below). Finally, lift the panes into the tracks and check that they slide freely from side to side.

How to fit door and window locks

Security is important in any home. Do not leave windows open when you go out and always double lock your front door. By fitting locks to all doors and windows, you will not only deter burglars but also reduce your home insurance premiums.

Doors

A mortise deadlock is very secure. The body of the mortise lock actually fits inside the door, shooting its bolt into a recess cut in the edge of the door frame. In order to overcome such a lock, a burglar would have to destroy the door around it.

Fitting a mortise lock is more difficult than a basic spring-loaded rim latch, since you must cut a slot in the door for its body, and that slot must only just be wide enough otherwise you run the risk of weakening the door. Normally, the bulk of the slot is cut by boring a series of holes into the door edge with a brace and bit, or flat bit in a power drill, then cleaning up the sides with a chisel.

Mortise locks should always comply with British Standard BS3621 and have a five-lever movement. Each of the lock's five operating levers has a cut-out that corresponds to the shape of the key; if only one doesn't match, the lock can't be opened. This makes them safe from lock picks and skeleton keys.

1

Mark the height of the lock body on the edge of the door; then mark the depth of on both faces.

2

Drill a series of holes into the edge of the door with a swing brace and auger bit; mark the depth of hole on the bit with adhesive tape.

3

After chiselling out the mortise and checking for fit (with bolt extended to assist removal), mark the keyhole with a bradawl.

4

Cut the keyhole with a padsaw after drilling right through the door into a block of wood to prevent the surface from splitting.

Lock bars and rack bolts

An alternative to the traditional door chain, which prevents a bogus caller forcing the door open, but allows you to open it sufficiently to identify him, is the lock bar or door limiter. The pivotting, cast metal bar screws to the door frame and engages with a bracket screwed to the door. When connected, the bar limits the amount by which the door can be opened. To open the door fully, you must first close it so that the pegs on the door bracket can be disengaged from their slots in the bar.

The rack bolt is a more secure alternative to the ordinary surface-mounted bolt. It fits into a hole drilled in the edge of the door and is operated by a splined key from inside, the bolt shooting into a hole in the door frame. Smaller versions are made for windows.

Windows

It is also essential to lock up the windows, even those upstairs.

Locks for metal windows are invariably held in place by self-tapping screws, but make sure the locks you buy have the right screws for the frame material — steel windows will need a different type of screw to aluminium ones.

Cockspur handle locks are usually in the form of a sliding bolt screwed to the fixed frame. When the cockspur handle is in the closed position, the bolt is slid up beneath its nose and locked to prevent the handle being turned.

Stay locks may be in the form of a clamp that fits round the stay and rest, or a sliding bolt, which attaches to the stay and can be locked beneath the rest. The latter type occupies some of the holes in the stay.

Fitting a lock bar into a recess cut in the door frame; make sure that the screws grip firmly into solid wood.

After opening a cockspur handle lock and drilling pilot holes, screw the staple to the frame with self-tapping screws.

TIP 101

How to 'green' your home

In recent years there has been growing evidence that the burning of fossil fuels is contributing to the problem of global warming; likewise, burying waste in landfill sites is not only a pollutant, it is also a waste of resources that could be recycled. There are myriad ways you can help to save energy around the home, thereby reducing your impact on the environment, and helping to save money too. Study the diagram on these pages and get inspired to 'green your home' today.

Secondary glazing

Energy-efficient light bulbs

Thermostatic radiator valves

Double glazing

Cavity-wall insulation

Room thermostats

Triple glazing

Cavity-wall insulation

Programmer for central heating

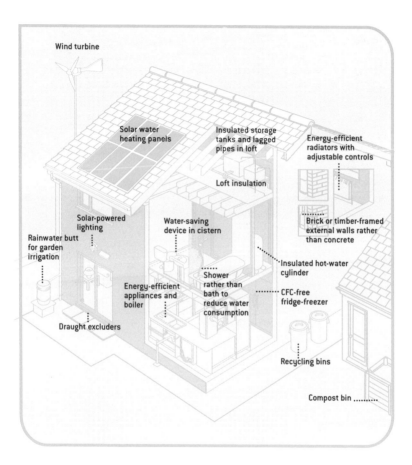

Wind turbine

Solar water
heating panels

Insulated storage
tanks and lagged
pipes in loft

Energy-efficient
radiators with
adjustable controls

Loft insulation

Solar-powered
lighting

Water-saving
device in cistern

Brick or timber-framed
external walls rather
than concrete

Rainwater butt
for garden
irrigation

Insulated hot-water
cylinder

Shower
rather than
bath to
reduce water
consumption

CFC-free
fridge-freezer

Energy-efficient
appliances and
boiler

Draught excluders

Recycling bins

Compost bin

SAFETY

DIY is hugely rewarding but it can be hazardous. Working on raised platforms or ladders holds inherent risks, many DIY tools can cause severe injuries if used without due care and attention and, as already noted, careless work with electrics can be fatal. Read the following advice and ensure that all your DIY projects are carried out sensibly and safely.

Ladder safety

Ladders should be placed at ground level 1m (3ft) away from the wall for every 4m (12ft) of height. The top of the ladder should overlap the highest point and should be tied in place if possible. Secure at the base with a sandbag, or tie it to wooden pegs knocked into the ground. If the ground is soggy, place the ladder on a board to make sure it's secure.

A tower platform, available from hire shops, makes exterior decorating easier if your house is large, but never climb down the side, which will unbalance it. Special designs are available for chalet bungalows, wide bay windows or houses that have roofs on several levels.

Electricity

HOUSE WIRING

Faults in wiring cause 2,200 fires and about ten deaths per year in Britain.

➜ You should have your household wiring checked every five years. This may sound excessive, but the cost is a small price to pay for electrical safety.

➜ If your wiring circuits are more than 25 years old, or if your sockets are of the round, two-pin type you almost certainly need to renew them. Before checking or repairing wiring sockets or switches, turn off the power at the mains switch.

➜ Get expert help for all repairs and wiring. If you think there may be a fault, immediately contact an approved contractor.

➜ Always keep a torch handy in case it is needed during a power cut.

PLUGS AND FLEXES

Faulty flexes cause 1,000 fires and several deaths per year.

➜ Always buy shatter-proof plugs that meet BS 1363 or BS 1363/A, which are stronger than most. Make sure the clamp in the plug properly grips the outer plastic cover of the flex and not just the leads.

➜ Wire colour codes:
  Live = Brown
  Neutral = Blue
  Earth = Yellow/Green

→ Don't overload plug sockets. Use adaptors as little as possible. Ideally, you should use a separate socket for every appliance, but this is not always possible. If you regularly use two appliances from one point, fit a double socket.
→ Make sure you are using the correct fuse for the appliance.

Fire

No one should underrate the danger of fire. In this country every year there are about 50,000 accidental fires in the home, which kill about 800 people and injure over 14,000 others.

SMOKE ALARMS

Over 60 per cent of households now have a smoke alarm. Your chances of surviving a fire are two to three times greater if you have one fitted. Battery-operated models cost from as little as £4. You can also buy mains-powered alarms if you have a large house and need several alarms. You should preferably have one on each floor of the house.

Once you have fitted a smoke alarm, it is easy to forget about it. But it is important to maintain it properly: it could save your life.

→ Make a note in your diary to replace the battery at least once a year.
→ Test the battery once a week.
→ Vacuum dust from inside the alarm.
→ Test the sensor annually by waving a smoking candle under it.

DIY safety

One of the biggest causes of home accidents is the enthusiastic DIYer who overlooks the essential precautions when using power tools, hazardous chemicals or even climbing a ladder.

→ Never cut corners, always use the right tool for the job and keep tools in good working order.
→ When drilling walls, avoid areas adjacent to power sockets and the area at right angles and vertically above them. Power cables are usually routed in these locations.
→ Always take care of hands when working, and wear gloves whenever possible.
→ Always wear protective clothing – face masks, safety goggles, ear defenders or knee pads – when undertaking jobs that may be dangerous or harmful.
→ Prepare yourself and your working area properly before you begin.
→ Fuels, glue, cleaners, paints and lubricants all contain chemicals that can be harmful. Always follow the makers' safety guidelines. Ensure that you have adequate ventilation.
→ Use residual circuit breaker devices when operating power tools.
→ Put blade covers on knives and chisels when not using them.
→ Keep children away from all DIY work.

THE BUILDING REGULATIONS

The building regulations are based on the notion that buildings have to be built to minimum quality standards. The first incarnation of building regulations was introduced after the Great Plague of 1665 and the Great Fire of London that followed it, in 1666. It was determined that buildings should be built to minimum standards of fire safety and hygiene to prevent such catastrophes happening again. Their scope has extended from just fire safety and hygiene to include both public and private health and safety in and around buildings, disabled access, pollution and noise control, ventilation, energy conservation and more.

What are you allowed to do?

In England and Wales the building regulations are broken down into 14 parts, each of which has an 'Approved Document' that sets out example details and diagrams, which explain minimum compliance. In Northern Ireland there is a slightly different system, and in Scotland there is the 'Building Warrant' system, which sets out seven sections and three appendices. Speaking in broad terms, however, the systems are the same. Here follows a brief list of each of the 14 sections of the building regulations for England and Wales.

A STRUCTURE

It is a cornerstone of the regulations that the structure of buildings should be sound, safe and suitable for their purpose. Even if you have no need for the full plans application, you will have to provide a set of written calculations to prove that the structural proposals have been worked out correctly.

B FIRE SAFETY

This part of the building regulations was set out to prevent buildings from spreading fires from one house to the next. The regulations require that any habitable room, with a floor more than 4.5sq m (15sq ft) above ground level (second floor and above, generally), must have a direct protected route to the exit (usually the front door) without passing through any other habitable rooms. A 'habitable room' includes a bedroom or living room, whereas a storage area or bathroom is not counted. If you plan to convert your loft, and you have an open-plan ground floor leading to the front door, you may find that you need to think again.

C SITE PREPARATION – RESISTANCE TO CONTAMINANTS AND MOISTURE

This section rarely causes problems for homeowner projects, but comes under close scrutiny with basement projects. There are several very different ways of going about the tanking and waterproofing of a basement, and different specialists can often give conflicting advice.

D TOXIC SUBSTANCES

This section covers a whole range of items but asbestos tends to be the headline issue.

E RESISTANCE TO THE PASSAGE OF SOUND

This section can become a major issue for new-build flats, terraced and semidetached houses, and for conversions of buildings where two or more dwellings are created. The regulations now require that the building should be sound-tested on completion to prove compliance.

F VENTILATION

Habitable rooms, such as bedrooms,

need a slot in the windowframe to allow trickle ventilation. Bathrooms, shower-rooms and WCs that do not have a window must have suitable mechanical ventilation that extracts air at a minimum number of litres per second and achieves a certain number of air changes per hour. Construction also needs ventilation, with spaces being required between layers of roofs, to prevent the build-up of condensation, and below raised floors to keep damp at bay.

G HYGIENE

For homeowner projects, this section is really about commonsense. If basic methods and fixtures are used in the standard way, there are very rarely any issues of compliance under section G.

H DRAINAGE AND WASTE DISPOSAL

The big issues here tend to be about the horizontal distances and gradients of waste pipes and drains, both above and below ground. If you are connecting to an existing drain, it is not unusual for the building inspector to require a survey. This can be done using a specialist CCTV camera in the drain to see if there are any cracks or imperfections.

J COMBUSTION APPLIANCES AND FUEL STORAGE

The correct ventilation for gas appliances is vital to ensure that poisonous carbon monoxide gas, and other such pollutants, do not build up in a way that could be dangerous. This part of the regulations also deals with chimneys and flues, hearths, sizes for fireplaces, the storage of heating oil, and other such matters.

K PROTECTION FROM FALLING, COLLISION AND IMPACT

The design of staircases, guardings, balustrades and handrails are all covered in this section. There are very helpful diagrams to explain the minimum standards of what can be quite complicated requirements. In particular, the regulations explain what must be done with tapering treads on a spiral stair, or the winding treads on a turn of a staircase. This section also sets out provisions to prevent collisions by preventing windows from projecting into the path of pedestrians, and ensuring that doors that swing both ways have vision panels.

L CONSERVATION OF FUEL AND POWER

The amendment to part L of the regulations that came into force in April 2006 has caused great consternation and confusion ever since. The reason for the consternation is that it threatened to prevent people from doing precisely what so many people want to do, which is to extend their house, with lots of glass in the walls and roof. The reason for the confusion is that there are three different ways to calculate what you might be allowed to do. These calculations are fiendishly difficult, leaving many people not knowing what

they can and cannot do. Often the best way through this matter is to engage a specialist surveyor.

M ACCESS AND FACILITIES FOR DISABLED PEOPLE

New works must have level access to the entry level of the building, and must have a suitable WC facility on that level too. This should be suitable for an ambulant disabled person rather than a wheelchair-bound person. Staircases may have to comply with regulations for disabled people, with regard to the amount of risers, gradient and stair nosings.

N GLAZING – IMPACT, OPENING AND CLEANING SAFETY

This section introduces requirements for 'manifestation', which involves markings on the surface of the glass in glass doors, so that people will realise that the doors are shut. This part also outlines the need for specially strengthened glass in doors and areas adjacent to them, and also minimum standards for the consideration of how glass may be cleaned safely.

P ELECTRICAL SAFETY

The most recent additional section to the regulations, part P, was brought in to combat the dangers of DIY electrical work in people's homes. Now, anything more than the simplest repairs must be done by a qualified electrician who can certify that the work has been done to the necessary standard.

INDEX